This Book belongs to

LEISURE ARTS, INC.
Little Rock, Arkansas

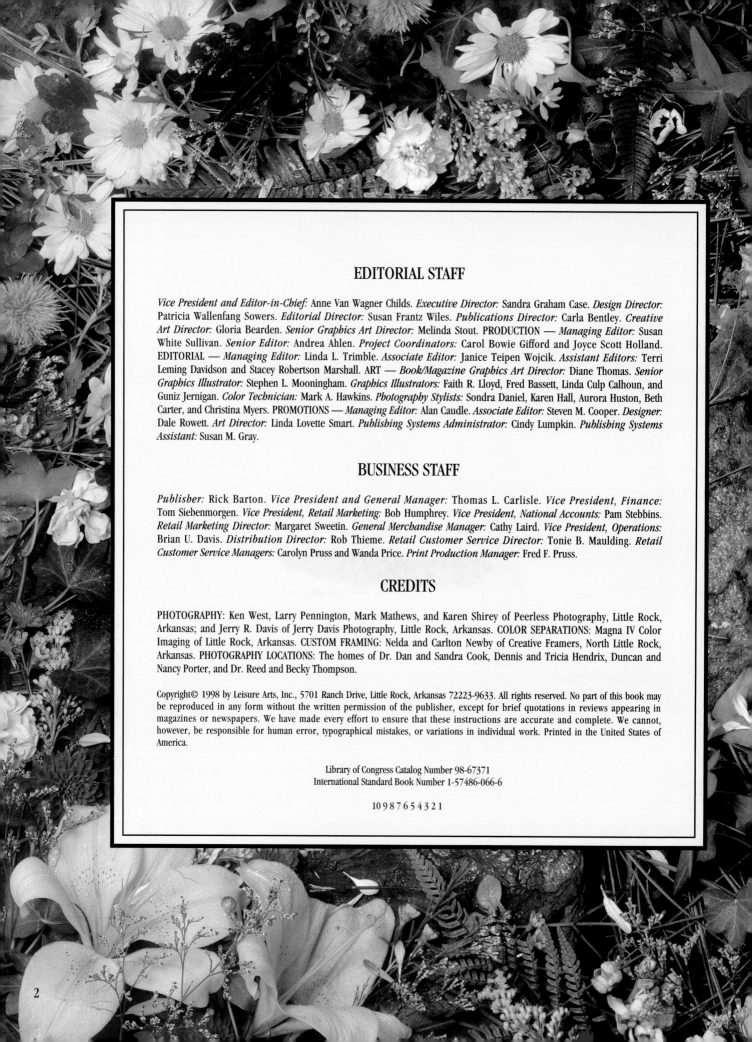

EDITORIAL STAFF

Vice President and Editor-in-Chief: Anne Van Wagner Childs. *Executive Director:* Sandra Graham Case. *Design Director:* Patricia Wallenfang Sowers. *Editorial Director:* Susan Frantz Wiles. *Publications Director:* Carla Bentley. *Creative Art Director:* Gloria Bearden. *Senior Graphics Art Director:* Melinda Stout. PRODUCTION — *Managing Editor:* Susan White Sullivan. *Senior Editor:* Andrea Ahlen. *Project Coordinators:* Carol Bowie Gifford and Joyce Scott Holland. EDITORIAL — *Managing Editor:* Linda L. Trimble. *Associate Editor:* Janice Teipen Wojcik. *Assistant Editors:* Terri Leming Davidson and Stacey Robertson Marshall. ART — *Book/Magazine Graphics Art Director:* Diane Thomas. *Senior Graphics Illustrator:* Stephen L. Mooningham. *Graphics Illustrators:* Faith R. Lloyd, Fred Bassett, Linda Culp Calhoun, and Guniz Jernigan. *Color Technician:* Mark A. Hawkins. *Photography Stylists:* Sondra Daniel, Karen Hall, Aurora Huston, Beth Carter, and Christina Myers. PROMOTIONS — *Managing Editor:* Alan Caudle. *Associate Editor:* Steven M. Cooper. *Designer:* Dale Rowett. *Art Director:* Linda Lovette Smart. *Publishing Systems Administrator:* Cindy Lumpkin. *Publishing Systems Assistant:* Susan M. Gray.

BUSINESS STAFF

Publisher: Rick Barton. *Vice President and General Manager:* Thomas L. Carlisle. *Vice President, Finance:* Tom Siebenmorgen. *Vice President, Retail Marketing:* Bob Humphrey. *Vice President, National Accounts:* Pam Stebbins. *Retail Marketing Director:* Margaret Sweetin. *General Merchandise Manager:* Cathy Laird. *Vice President, Operations:* Brian U. Davis. *Distribution Director:* Rob Thieme. *Retail Customer Service Director:* Tonie B. Maulding. *Retail Customer Service Managers:* Carolyn Pruss and Wanda Price. *Print Production Manager:* Fred F. Pruss.

CREDITS

PHOTOGRAPHY: Ken West, Larry Pennington, Mark Mathews, and Karen Shirey of Peerless Photography, Little Rock, Arkansas; and Jerry R. Davis of Jerry Davis Photography, Little Rock, Arkansas. COLOR SEPARATIONS: Magna IV Color Imaging of Little Rock, Arkansas. CUSTOM FRAMING: Nelda and Carlton Newby of Creative Framers, North Little Rock, Arkansas. PHOTOGRAPHY LOCATIONS: The homes of Dr. Dan and Sandra Cook, Dennis and Tricia Hendrix, Duncan and Nancy Porter, and Dr. Reed and Becky Thompson.

Library of Congress Catalog Number 98-67371
International Standard Book Number 1-57486-066-6

10 9 8 7 6 5 4 3 2 1

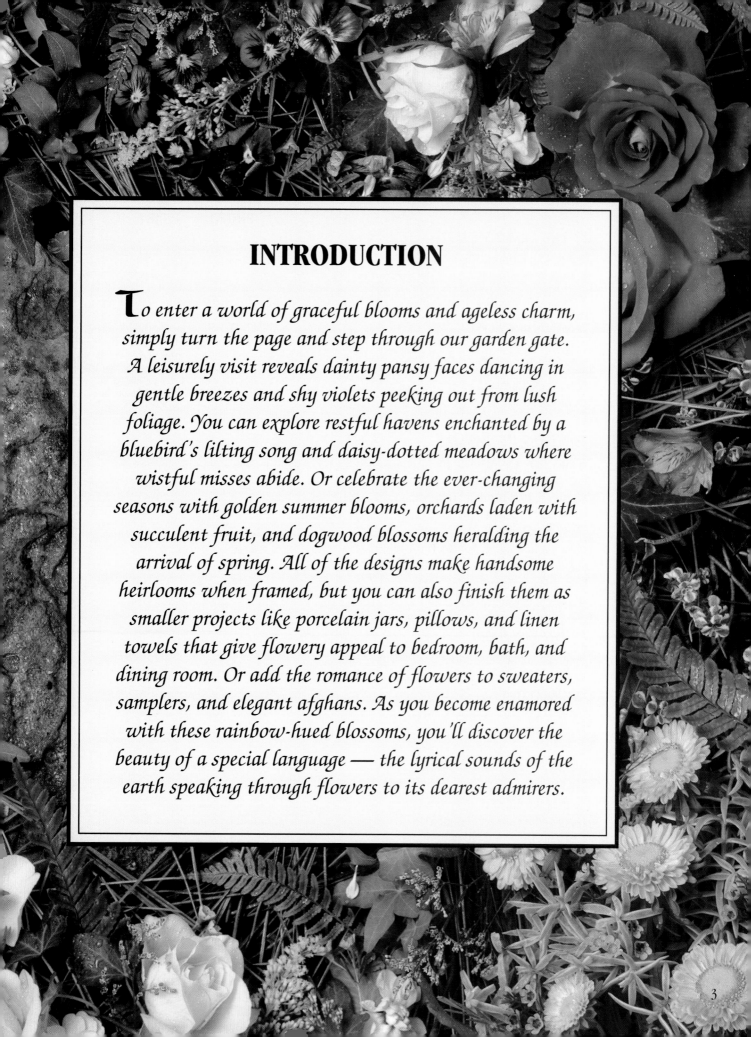

INTRODUCTION

To enter a world of graceful blooms and ageless charm, simply turn the page and step through our garden gate. A leisurely visit reveals dainty pansy faces dancing in gentle breezes and shy violets peeking out from lush foliage. You can explore restful havens enchanted by a bluebird's lilting song and daisy-dotted meadows where wistful misses abide. Or celebrate the ever-changing seasons with golden summer blooms, orchards laden with succulent fruit, and dogwood blossoms heralding the arrival of spring. All of the designs make handsome heirlooms when framed, but you can also finish them as smaller projects like porcelain jars, pillows, and linen towels that give flowery appeal to bedroom, bath, and dining room. Or add the romance of flowers to sweaters, samplers, and elegant afghans. As you become enamored with these rainbow-hued blossoms, you'll discover the beauty of a special language — the lyrical sounds of the earth speaking through flowers to its dearest admirers.

TABLE OF CONTENTS

AT THE GARDEN GATE

*G*listening in the morning sun with the splendor of fine gems, the garden beckons to all. A gentle touch on the latch opens the gate to reveal a paradise of grace and beauty. Enter joyfully into this sanctuary, which is adorned with thriving greenery and well-tended blossoms. With senses attuned to twitters and fragrances, textures and hues, discover the buoyant spirit of happiness that envelops visitors who respond to the garden's irresistible call.

Charts on pages 48-50

To cultivate a garden is to walk with God, to go hand in hand with nature in some of her most beautiful processes.

— CHRISTIAN NESTELL BOVEE

8

Charts on pages 51-53

THE DAISY GIRL

Boundless fields of waving wildflowers have held an irresistible appeal for wee lasses throughout the ages. Blending innocence and fresh, natural beauty, a delicate young miss gathering a sunny bouquet becomes a winsome flower girl attending the marriage of a lush, verdant meadow and a cloud-laced summer sky.

And all the meadows, wide unrolled,
Were green and silver, green and gold,
Where buttercups and daisies spun
Their shining tissues in the sun.

— JULIA C.R. DORR

Charts on pages 54-56

PICTURESQUE PANSIES

With their delicate heads bobbing
in the breeze, congenial pansies bring
animated charm to the garden. Clusters
of these vivacious flowers mix and mingle
like beautiful young ladies telling tales
over tea. Brightly colored butterflies,
attracted to the sweet-scented blooms,
act as admiring suitors courting
the fairest of the fair.

Charts on pages 62-63

15

here's rosemary, that's for remembrance; . . . and there is pansies, that's for thoughts.

— WILLIAM SHAKESPEARE

Chart on pages 64-65

Known in simpler times as heartsease and love-in-idleness, pretty pansies have retained their ranking as sentimental favorites. Symbolizing love and kind thoughts, a profusion of these delicate beauties brighten bath accessories and join in a heartwarming circle on a cozy coverlet.

Charts on pages 63-65

Chart on page 63

IN THE ORCHARD

Delivered fresh from Mother Nature's abundant pantry, tantalizing fruits arrive in ripe, rosy condition. The enduring recipe for these sweet treasures blends a fairyland of blossoms with a wealth of sun, showers, and rich soil. Blessed with a bountiful harvest, we celebrate our good fortune on a peachy coverlet and a tastefully framed portrait of plums.

Charts on pages 66-67

Paradise is not wholly gone; rich morsels of precious fruitage still reward the man of well-directed toil.

— PRESBYTERIAN WITNESS

Charts on pages 66, 68, and 69

SONG
OF THE
BLUEBIRD

Buoyant as the breath of spring,
the bluebird's song heralds the arrival
of delightful dogwood blossoms and
tiny bird eggs. An enraptured innocent
finds bliss in a lovely arbor with
this rose-breasted bird.

Charts on pages 58

*S*erene and quiet, a cozy corner can refresh the soul. Become engrossed in an intriguing book while lounging in your heavenly hideaway. Or contemplate the miraculous mingling of celestial and earthbound wonders as you watch graceful songbirds explore the loveliness of delicate blossoms.

Chart on page 60

Chart on page 60

Chart on page 57

AS
MONTHS
GO BY

Each season brings its own special blessings and beauties. Winter begins the cycle with the awesome wonder of a world cloaked in white, while spring welcomes new life with an explosion of blossoms and blooms. Then lush summer days ripen into abundant autumn harvests wrapped in earthy hues. As months go by, we revel in the mysteries of these ever-changing seasons.

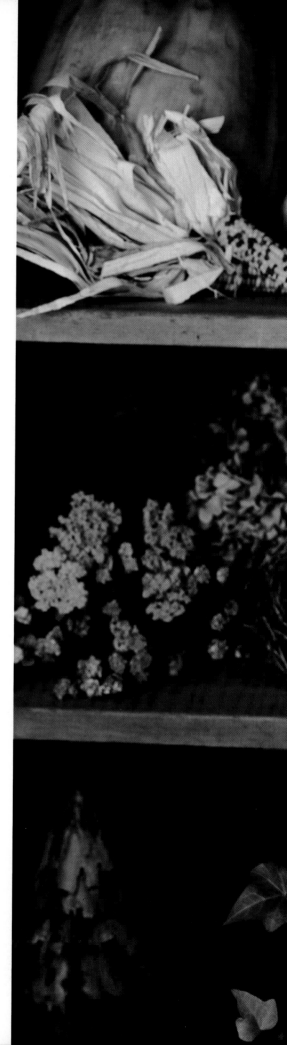

Chart on pages 70-71

27

Nature gives to every time and
season some beauties of its own; and
from morning to night, as from the cradle
to the grave, is but a succession of
changes so gentle and easy that we can
scarcely mark their progress.

— CHARLES DICKENS

Charts on pages 72-75

GARDEN OF INNOCENCE

Dainty and shy, violets are fitting
choices for a garden of young innocents.
Richly clothed in purple, these fair flowers
glance out from their foliage like youngsters
peeking from behind their mothers' skirts.
And like our little lads and lasses, violets
hold secret delights for those who pause
to appreciate their happy, wholesome
faces and refreshing sweetness.

Charts on pages 92-94

GOLDEN SUMMER DAYS

On dreamy summer afternoons, when time travels at a gentler pace, the air seems to glisten with golden tones. These long days of nourishing radiance produce an award-winning sampling of nature's most splendid decor. Cheerful sunflowers and a carefree butterfly add the warm hues of these idyllic days to your home.

Charts on page 78

The glorious sun, stays in his course and plays the alchemist, turning with splendour of his precious eye the meagre cloddy earth to glittering gold.

— WILLIAM SHAKESPEARE

Chart on pages 76-77

35

Chart on page 79

Chart on page 78

*K*issed with the allure of nature, butterflies are one of God's most fragile yet wondrous creations. Gracing field and flower for a mere moment in time, they charm us with their lilting, capricious flight. Add sunny enchantment to your decor by displaying these winged treasures along with radiant summer flora.

Chart on page 78

ROSE GARDEN TEA

One of the closest things to heaven on earth is a balmy afternoon spent sipping tea in a rose garden. Endowed with fragrance and ambience, this exquisite retreat becomes the setting for a ceremony that refreshes both body and soul. Honor such a blissful occasion with dewy roses on an elegant afghan and on a lovely framed teacup.

Charts on pages 80-81 and 83

*Every rose is an autograph
from the hand of the Almighty God
on this world about us.*

— THEODORE PARKER

Chart on pages 80-81

For a peaceful haven that promises to breathe new life into your spirit, combine blushing roses, aromatic tea, and a sweet-smelling garden. Add refinement to the tea table with heirloom-quality linens, and bring a touch of nostalgia to your dining area with a young miss at play in her rose arbor.

Charts on pages 82-83

Chart on pages 84-85

EARTH SPEAKS IN FLOWERS

Ever alive, the Earth finds ways to speak to those who listen. It reveals itself in the ocean's roar, in gently murmuring spring rains, and in the wind whispering softly in the trees. But Mother Nature sends her most sentimental messages through flowers. Dewy buds and blossoms capture the dawn's rays, translating them into a million multicolored syllables. The warming day turns their luminous petals into a heavenly love song that is hushed to a lingering lullaby at eventide.

Charts on pages 86-90

When flowers speak, they spell out our deepest joys and truest loves in all the colors of the rainbow. Lustrous petals are shaped into radiant nosegays that express feelings and thoughts beyond the range of spoken words. These delicate inscribed bouquets reveal heartfelt sentiments on a lacy pillow, and flowery monograms add a personal touch to our precious treasures.

Charts on pages 86 and 88

Charts on pages 86-89

Charts on pages 86-87 and 89

AT THE GARDEN GATE

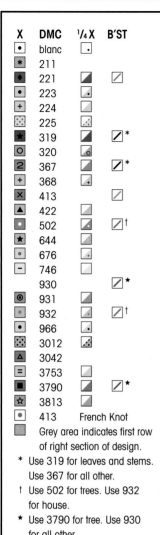

X	DMC	¼ X	B'ST
•	blanc	•	
*	211		
◆	221	◢	�%✏
•	223	◢	
+	224	◢	
░	225	◢	
★	319	◢	◢ *
O	320	◢	◢ *
2	367	◢	◢ *
+	368	◢	
✕	413		◢
▲	422	◢	
◉	502	◢	◢ †
★	644	◢	
●	676	◢	
–	746	◢	
	930		◢ *
◉	931	◢	
◉	932	◢	◢ †
•	966	◢	
▨	3012	◢	
▲	3042		
=	3753	◢	
▦	3790	◢	◢ *
☆	3813	◢	
◉	413	French Knot	

Grey area indicates first row of right section of design.

* Use 319 for leaves and stems. Use 367 for all other.

† Use 502 for trees. Use 932 for house.

* Use 3790 for tree. Use 930 for all other.

STITCH COUNT (148w x 100h)

14 count	10⅝"	x	7¼"	
16 count	9¼"	x	6¼"	
18 count	8¼"	x	5⅝"	
22 count	6¾"	x	4⅝"	

"Touch but the Latch" in Frame (shown on page 7): The design was stitched over 2 fabric threads on a 17" x 14" piece of Cream Belfast Linen (32 ct). Two strands of floss were used for Cross Stitch and 1 strand for Backstitch and French Knots. Personalize and date design using alphabet and numerals provided. It was custom framed.

Design by Linda Gillum.

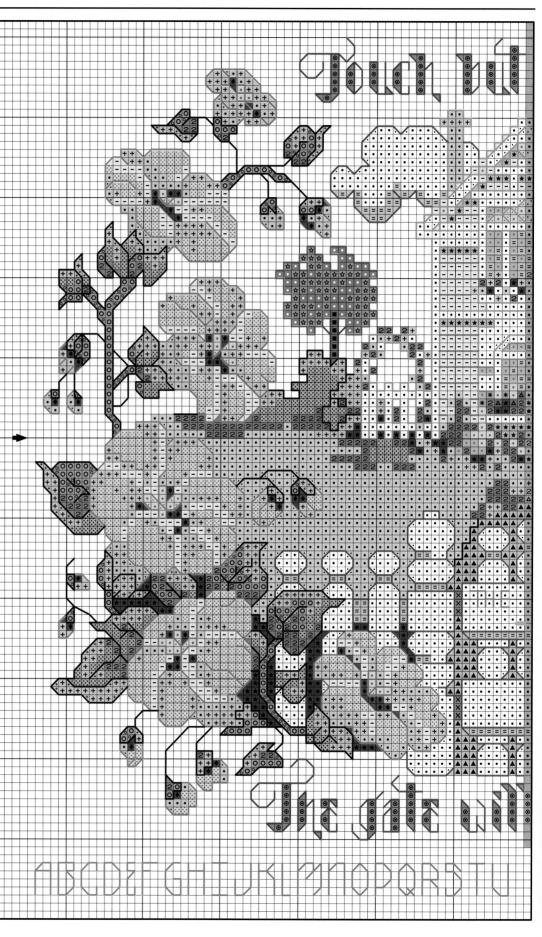

center name

center year

AT THE GARDEN GATE

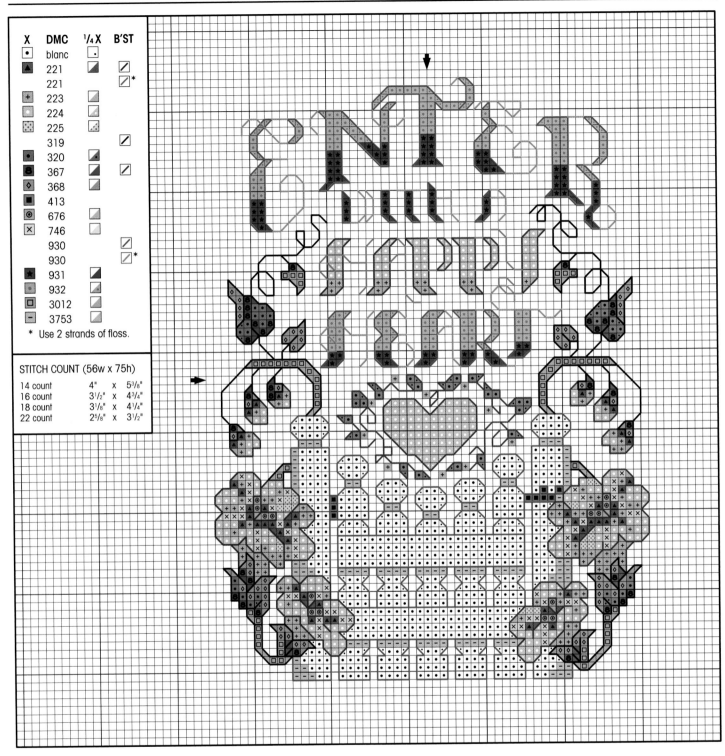

X	DMC	¼ X	B'ST
•	blanc	•	
▲	221	◢	◢
	221		◢*
+	223	◢	
⊡	224	◢	
⊡	225	◢	
	319		◢
●	320	◢	
◼	367	◢	◢
◇	368	◢	
◼	413		
⊙	676	◢	
✕	746	◢	
	930		◢
	930		◢*
★	931	◢	
●	932	◢	
□	3012	◢	
–	3753	◢	

* Use 2 strands of floss.

STITCH COUNT (56w x 75h)

14 count	4"	x	5³/₈"
16 count	3½"	x	4³/₄"
18 count	3¹/₈"	x	4¹/₄"
22 count	2⁵/₈"	x	3¹/₂"

"Enter with a Happy Heart" Wreath (shown on page 6): The design was stitched over 2 fabric threads on a 12" x 13" piece of Cream Belfast Linen (32 ct). Two strands of floss were used for Cross Stitch and 1 strand for Backstitch, unless otherwise noted in the color key.

For pillow, you will need a 5¹/₂" x 6³/₄" piece of fabric for pillow backing, 25" length of ¹/₄" dia. purchased cording with attached seam allowance, and polyester fiberfill.

Centering design, trim stitched piece to measure 5¹/₂" x 6³/₄".

If needed, trim seam allowances of cording to ¹/₂". Matching raw edges, pin cording to right side of stitched piece, making a ³/₈" clip in seam allowance of cording at corners. Ends of cording should overlap approximately 4". Turn

overlapped ends of cording toward outside edge of stitched piece; baste cording to stitched piece.

Matching right sides and raw edges, pin stitched piece and backing fabric together. Leaving an opening for turning, use a ¹/₂" seam allowance to sew pillow front and backing fabric together. Trim seam allowances diagonally at corners; turn pillow right side out, carefully pushing corners outward. Stuff pillow with polyester fiberfill and blind stitch opening closed. Attach to a decorated 12" dia. grapevine wreath.

Design by Linda Gillum.

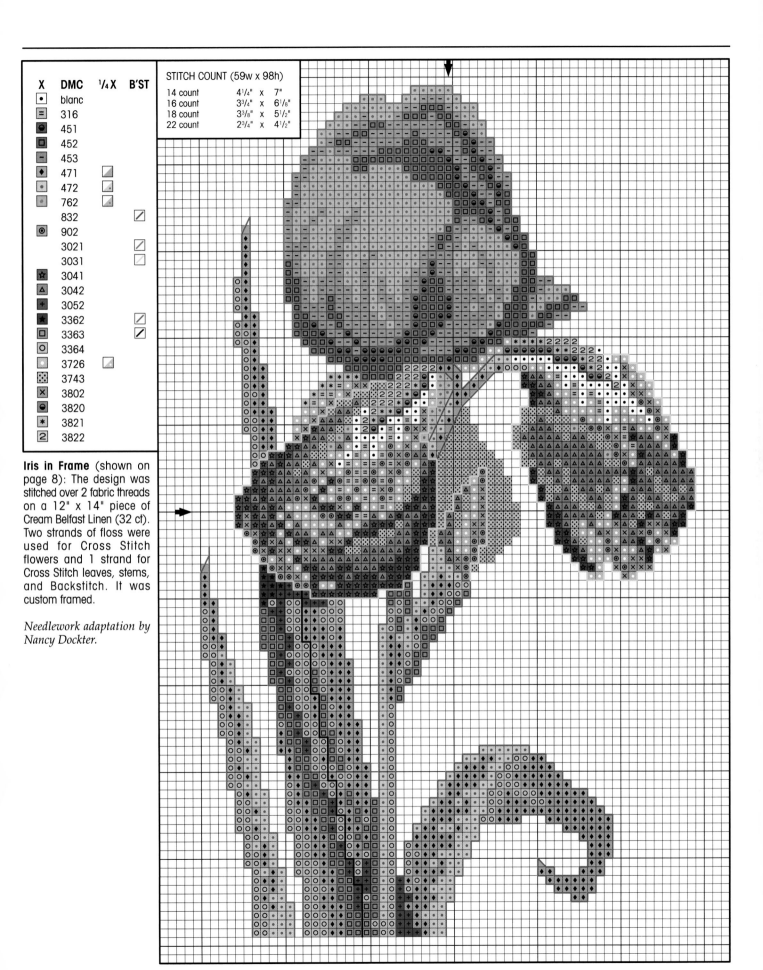

X	DMC	¼ X	B'ST
•	blanc		
=	316		
◉	451		
▣	452		
–	453		
◆	471	◢	
•	472	◢	
▪	762	◢	
	832		◢
◎	902		
	3021		◢
	3031		◢
☆	3041		
▲	3042		
✚	3052		
✦	3362		◢
▢	3363		◢
○	3364		
▫	3726	◢	
▨	3743		
✕	3802		
◕	3820		
✱	3821		
２	3822		

STITCH COUNT (59w x 98h)

	14 count	4¼" x 7"
	16 count	3¾" x 6⅛"
	18 count	3⅜" x 5½"
	22 count	2¾" x 4½"

Iris in Frame (shown on page 8): The design was stitched over 2 fabric threads on a 12" x 14" piece of Cream Belfast Linen (32 ct). Two strands of floss were used for Cross Stitch flowers and 1 strand for Cross Stitch leaves, stems, and Backstitch. It was custom framed.

Needlework adaptation by Nancy Dockter.

AT THE GARDEN GATE

X	DMC	¼ X	B'ST
•	blanc		
	310		╱
	451		╱
	470		
=	471		
•	472	◢	
◉	644		
◆	725		
○	746		
✳	783		
	922		╱
★	935		
◆	937		╱
✕	951		
◖	3031		
−	3032		
+	3051		
■	3078		
2	3362		
	3371		╱
△	3756		
◇	3781		

STITCH COUNT (81w x 98h)

14 count	5⅞"	x 7"
16 count	5⅛"	x 6⅛"
18 count	4½"	x 5½"
22 count	3¾"	x 4½"

White Narcissus in Frame (shown on page 9): The design was stitched over 2 fabric threads on a 13" x 14" piece of Cream Belfast Linen (32 ct). Two strands of floss were used for Cross Stitch flowers and 1 strand for Cross Stitch leaves and Backstitch. It was custom framed.

Needlework adaptation by Nancy Dockter.

STITCH COUNT (56w x 102h)

14 count	4"	x 7³⁄₈"
16 count	3¹⁄₂"	x 6³⁄₈"
18 count	3¹⁄₈"	x 5³⁄₄"
22 count	2⁵⁄₈"	x 4³⁄₄"

X	DMC	¹⁄₄ X	B'ST
	433		╱
■	610		
▲	611		
·	676	·	
▲	680	◢	
◉	721		
◆	725		
☆	726		
=	727		
○	729		
●	741		
−	742		
×	744		
	890		╱
★	3346		
□	3347		
●	3348	◢	
	3371		╱

Yellow Narcissus in Frame
(shown on page 8): The design was stitched over 2 fabric threads on a 12" x 14" piece of Cream Belfast Linen (32 ct). Two strands of floss were used for Cross Stitch flowers and 1 stand for Cross Stitch leaves and Backstitch. It was custom framed.

Needlework adaptation by Nancy Dockter.

53

THE DAISY GIRL

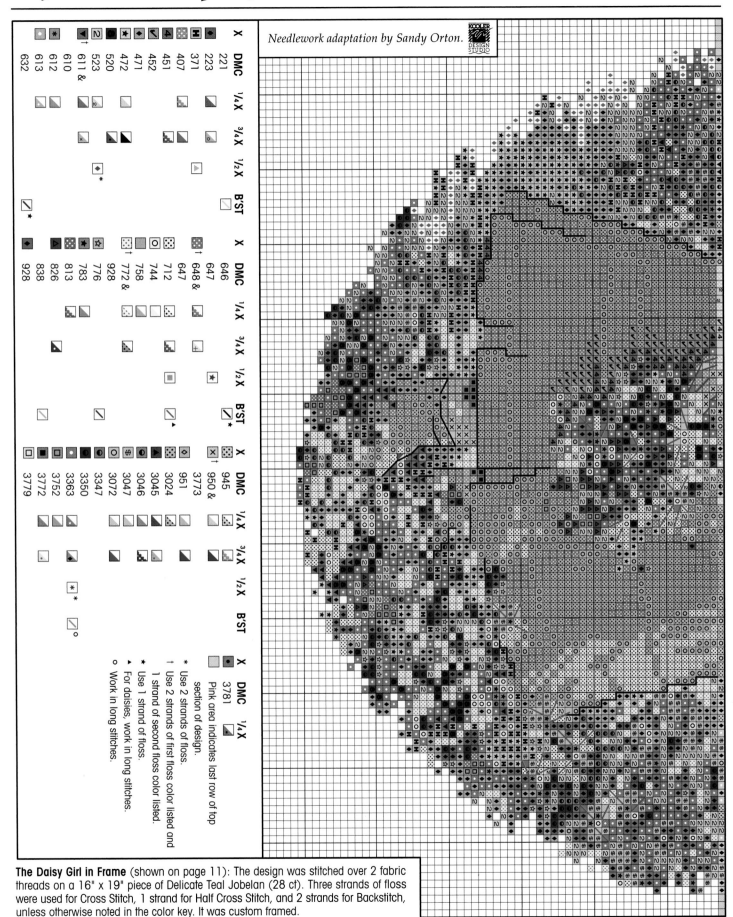

Needlework adaptation by Sandy Orton.

KOOLER DESIGN STUDIO

Color key — DMC floss numbers:

X DMC					
221	223	371	407	451	452
471	472	520	523	611 &	610
612	613	632			

X DMC					
646	647	648 &	647	712	744
758	772 &	776	928	838	826
813	783	928			

X DMC					
945	950 &	951	3773	3024	3045
3046	3047	3072	3347	3350	3363
3752	3772	3779			

X DMC	1/4X
3781	

Column headings: X · 1/4X · 3/4X · 1/2X · B'ST

* Use 2 strands of design.
* Use 2 strands of floss.
† Use 2 strands of first floss color listed and 1 strand of second floss color listed.
★ Use 1 strand of floss.
▶ For daisies, work in long stitches.
○ Work in long stitches.

Pink area indicates last row of top section of design.

The Daisy Girl in Frame (shown on page 11): The design was stitched over 2 fabric threads on a 16" x 19" piece of Delicate Teal Jobelan (28 ct). Three strands of floss were used for Cross Stitch, 1 strand for Half Cross Stitch, and 2 strands for Backstitch, unless otherwise noted in the color key. It was custom framed.

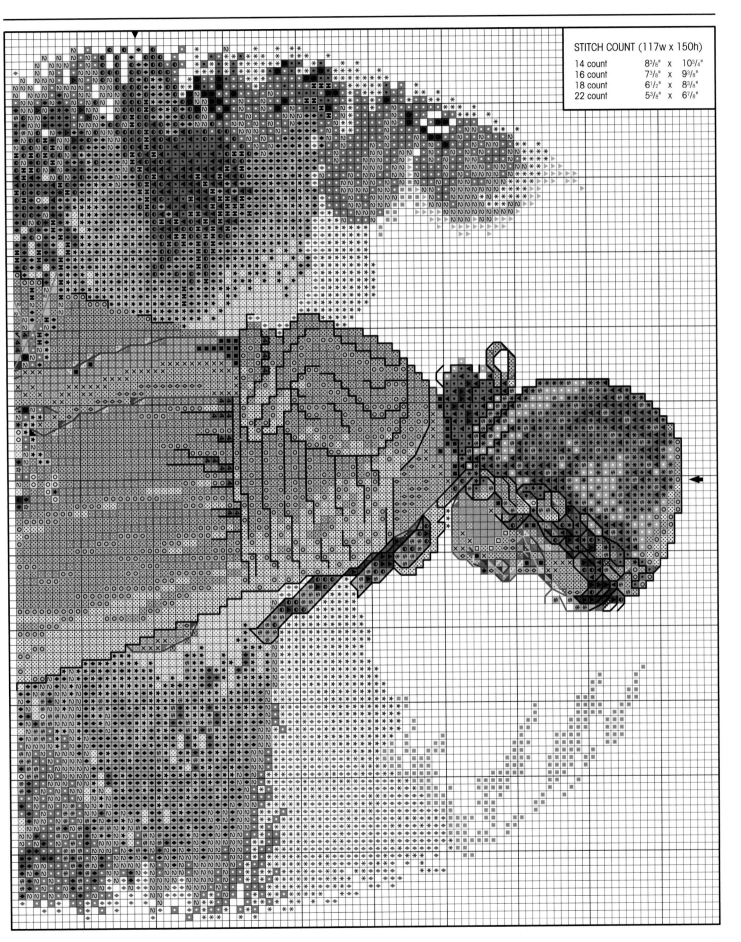

STITCH COUNT (117w x 150h)

count			
14 count	8³⁄₈"	x	10³⁄₄"
16 count	7³⁄₈"	x	9³⁄₈"
18 count	6¹⁄₂"	x	8³⁄₈"
22 count	5³⁄₈"	x	6⁷⁄₈"

the daisy girl

X	DMC	¼X	B'ST
•	blanc	•	
◉	561	◢	╱
	611		╱
▨	644	◢	
	646		╱
▣	712	◻	
◉	729	◢	
−	744		
⦁	822	◢	
▨	3022	◢	
+	3023	◻	
◉	3045	◢	
▲	3815	◢	
⦁	3816	◢	
☆	3817	◢	
⦁	3821	◢	╱

STITCH COUNT (46w x 75h)

14 count	3³⁄₈"	x	5³⁄₈"
16 count	2⁷⁄₈"	x	4³⁄₄"
18 count	2⁵⁄₈"	x	4¹⁄₄"
22 count	2¹⁄₈"	x	3¹⁄₂"

Daisy Bouquet Sweater
(shown on page 10): The design was stitched over an 8" x 10" piece of 12 mesh waste canvas on a purchased sweater. Three strands of floss were used for Cross Stitch and 1 strand for Backstitch. Refer to photo for placement of design on sweater.

Working on Waste Canvas: Waste canvas is a special canvas that provides an evenweave grid for placing stitches on fabric. After the design is worked over the canvas, the canvas threads are removed, leaving the design on the fabric. The canvas is available in several mesh sizes.

Cover edges of canvas with masking tape. Cut a piece of lightweight non-fusible interfacing the same size as canvas to provide a firm stitching base.

Find desired stitching area and mark center of area with a pin. Match center of canvas to pin. Use the blue threads in canvas to place canvas straight on garment; pin canvas to garment. Pin interfacing to wrong side of garment. Baste all layers together as shown in **Fig. 1**.

Using a sharp needle, work design, stitching from large holes to large holes. Trim canvas to within ³⁄₄" of design. Dampen canvas until it becomes limp. Pull out canvas threads one at a time using tweezers (**Fig. 2**). Trim interfacing close to design.

Fig. 1

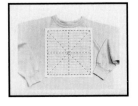

Fig. 2

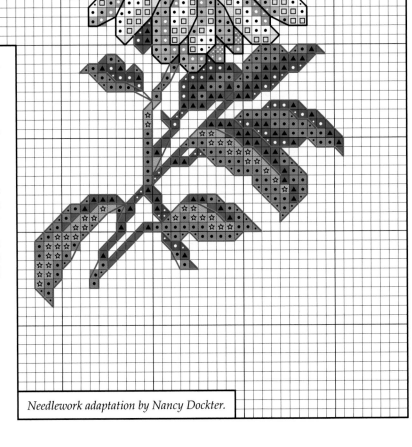

Needlework adaptation by Nancy Dockter.

SONG OF THE BLUEBIRD

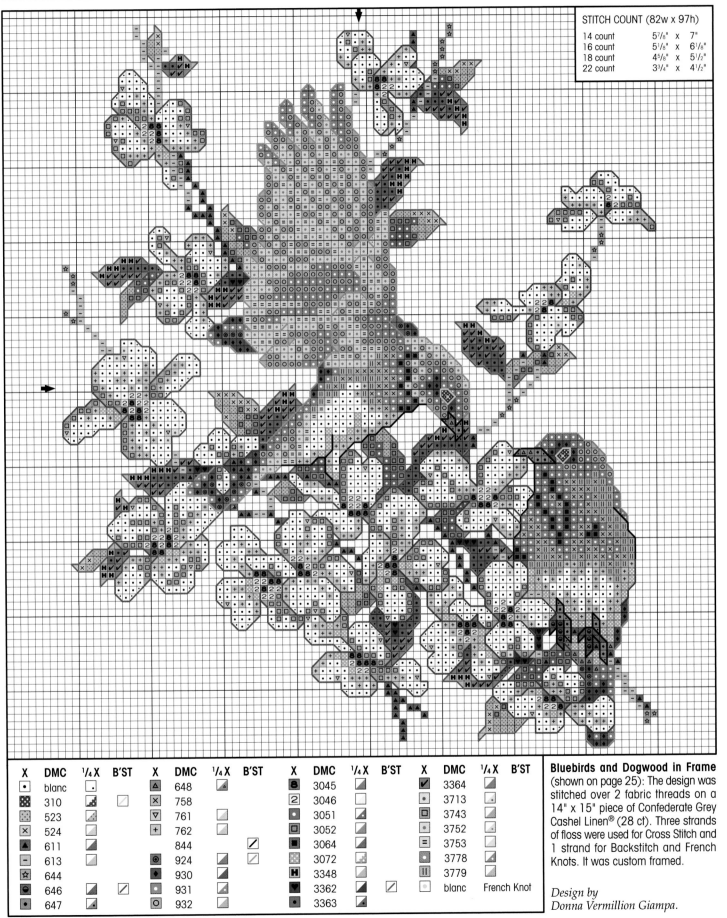

STITCH COUNT (82w x 97h)		
14 count	5⅞"	x 7"
16 count	5⅛"	x 6⅛"
18 count	4⅝"	x 5½"
22 count	3¾"	x 4½"

X	DMC	¼X	B'ST		X	DMC	¼X	B'ST		X	DMC	¼X	B'ST		X	DMC	¼X	B'ST
•	blanc	•			▲	648				▣	3045				✔	3364		
▨	310				✕	758				2	3046				•	3713		
▒	523				▽	761				▢	3051				▢	3743		
✕	524				+	762				▣	3052				•	3752		
▲	611					844				▨	3064				=	3753		
–	613				◉	924				▨	3072				•	3778		
☆	644				◆	930				H	3348				‖	3779		
▣	646				•	931				▼	3362				•	blanc		French Knot
•	647				◎	932				•	3363							

Bluebirds and Dogwood in Frame (shown on page 25): The design was stitched over 2 fabric threads on a 14" x 15" piece of Confederate Grey Cashel Linen® (28 ct). Three strands of floss were used for Cross Stitch and 1 strand for Backstitch and French Knots. It was custom framed.

Design by Donna Vermillion Giampa.

57

SONG OF THE BLUEBIRD

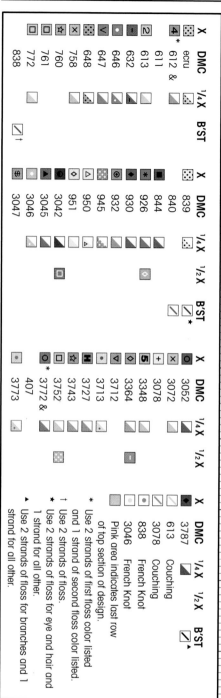

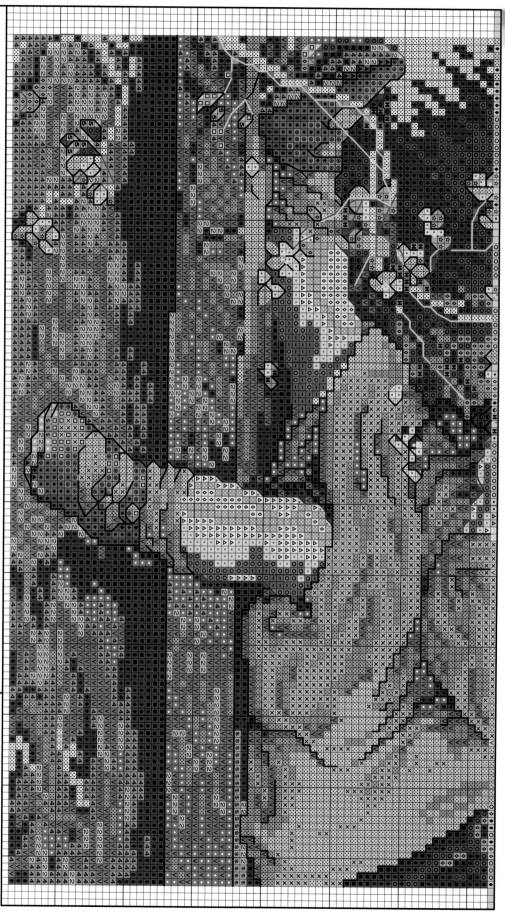

Song of the Bluebird in Frame (shown on page 23): The design was stitched over 2 fabric threads on a 17" x 19" piece of Confederate Grey Quaker Cloth (28 ct). Three strands of floss were used for Cross Stitch and 1 strand for Half Cross Stitch, Backstitch, and French Knots, unless otherwise noted in the color key. For Couching, 2 strands of floss were used for long Couching Stitch and 1 strand for tie-down Couching Stitch. See page 96, Stitch Diagrams. It was custom framed.

Needlework adaptation by Sandy Orton.

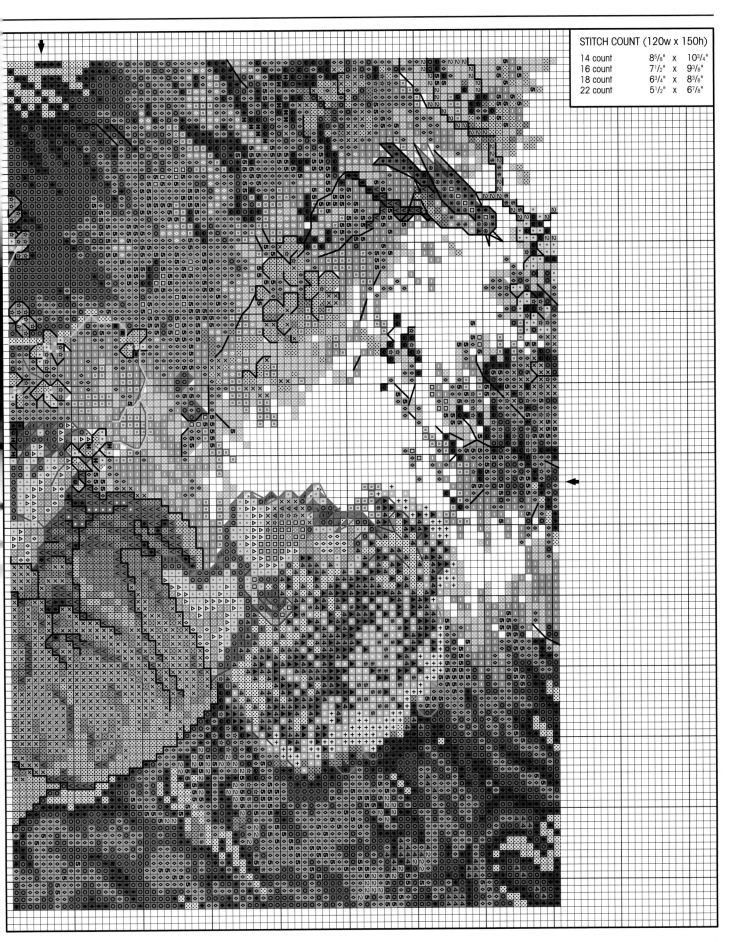

STITCH COUNT (120w x 150h)

14 count	8⅝"	x	10¾"
16 count	7½"	x	9⅜"
18 count	6¾"	x	8⅜"
22 count	5½"	x	6⅞"

SONG OF THE BLUEBIRD

X	DMC	¼ X	B'ST		X	DMC	¼ X	B'ST		X	DMC	¼ X	B'ST		X	DMC	¼ X	B'ST		X	DMC	¼ X	B'ST
•	blanc	•			•	644				☆	3046				□	3363				•	3041	French Knot
	523					646					3051				•	3364				* For Design #1, use 610. For
◆	524					648					3052				×	3713				Design #2, use 611.
	610		*		●	760				◆	3072					3727						
	611		*		•	761				+	3348				▲	3740						
–	613				•	3045				★	3362				○	3743						

60

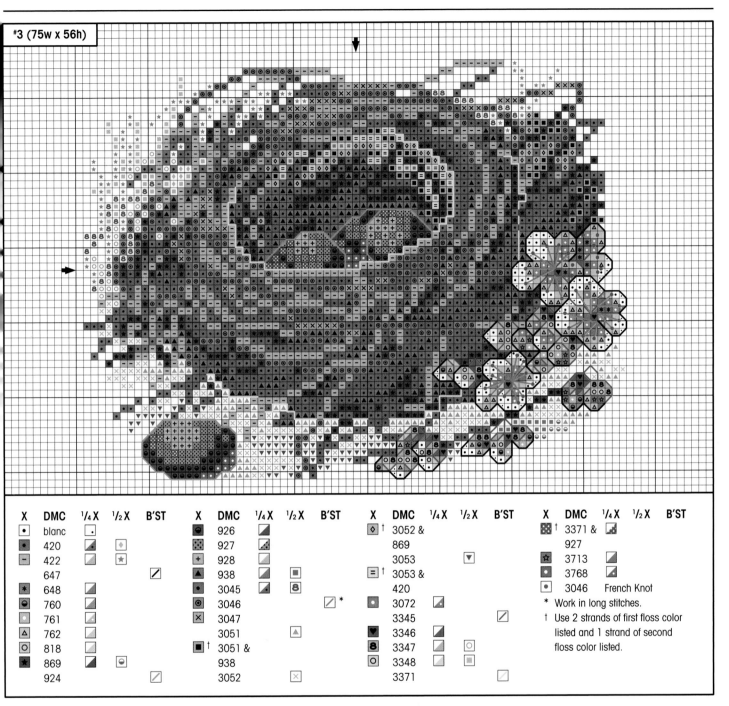

#3 (75w x 56h)

X	DMC	¼X	½X	B'ST	X	DMC	¼X	½X	B'ST	X	DMC	¼X	½X	B'ST	X	DMC	¼X	½X	B'ST
•	blanc					926				◇ †	3052 &				†	3371 &			
●	420		◆			927					869					927			
−	422		★		+	928					3053		▼		☆	3713			
	647				▲	938		■		= †	3053 &				▣	3768			
✱	648				●	3045		8			420				•	3046		French Knot	
◕	760				◉	3046			*	▣	3072				* Work in long stitches.				
▣	761				✕	3047					3345				† Use 2 strands of first floss color				
△	762					3051		▲		♥	3346				listed and 1 strand of second				
○	818				■ †	3051 &				8	3347		○		floss color listed.				
★	869		◔			938				○	3348		■						
	924					3052		✕			3371								

Dogwood Blossoms Bookmark (shown on page 24): Design #1 was stitched on a White Corner Marx-it™ bookmark (18 ct). Two strands of floss were used for Cross Stitch and 1 strand for Backstitch.

Heavenly Dogwood Pillow (shown on page 24): Design #2 was stitched over 2 fabric threads on a 14" x 13" piece of Confederate Grey Cashel Linen® (28 ct). Three strands of floss were used for Cross Stitch and 1 strand for Backstitch and French Knots.

For pillow, you will need an 8" x 7" piece of fabric for backing, 40" length of 2"w lace, and polyester fiberfill.

Centering design, trim stitched piece to measure 8" x 7".

For lace, press short edges of lace ½" to wrong side. Matching raw edges of stitched piece and bound edge of lace and mitering lace at corners, machine baste through all layers ½" from edges. Blind stitch mitered corners in place and pressed edges together.

Matching right sides and leaving an opening for turning, use a ½" seam allowance to sew stitched piece and backing fabric together. Trim seam allowances diagonally at corners; turn pillow right side out, carefully pushing corners outward. Stuff pillow with polyester fiberfill and blind stitch opening closed.

Designs by Donna Vermillion Giampa.

Bird Nest in Frame (shown on page 22): Design #3 was stitched over 2 fabric threads on a 13" x 12" piece of Confederate Grey Cashel Linen® (28 ct). Three strands of floss were used for Cross Stitch and 1 strand for Half Cross Stitch, Backstitch, and French Knots. It was custom framed.

Needlework adaptation by Donna Vermillion Giampa.

picturesque pansies

X	DMC	¼ X	B'ST
•	blanc		
⊙	315	◪	
2	316		
‖	471		
▫	742		
▨	743	◪	
○	744	◪	
•	745	◪	
−	746	◻	
H	831		
☆	832		
✕	833		
■	902	◪	◩
★	934		
	935		◩
=	938	◪	◩ *
8	987		
■	3031	◪	
▨	3345		
▦	3347		
	3371		◩
▨	3685	◪	
+	3687		
▣	3726	◪	
▽	3727		
◆	3803		
△	3822	◪	
⊙	938	French Knot	

* For antennae, work in long stitches.

STITCH COUNT (76w x 104h)

14 count	5½" x 7½"
16 count	4¾" x 6½"
18 count	4¼" x 5⅞"
22 count	3½" x 4¾"

Pansy Garden in Frame (shown on page 13): The design was stitched over 2 fabric threads on a 14" x 16" piece of Antique White Lugana (25 ct). Three strands of floss were used for Cross Stitch and 1 strand for Backstitch and French Knots. It was custom framed.

Needlework adaptation by Carol Emmer.

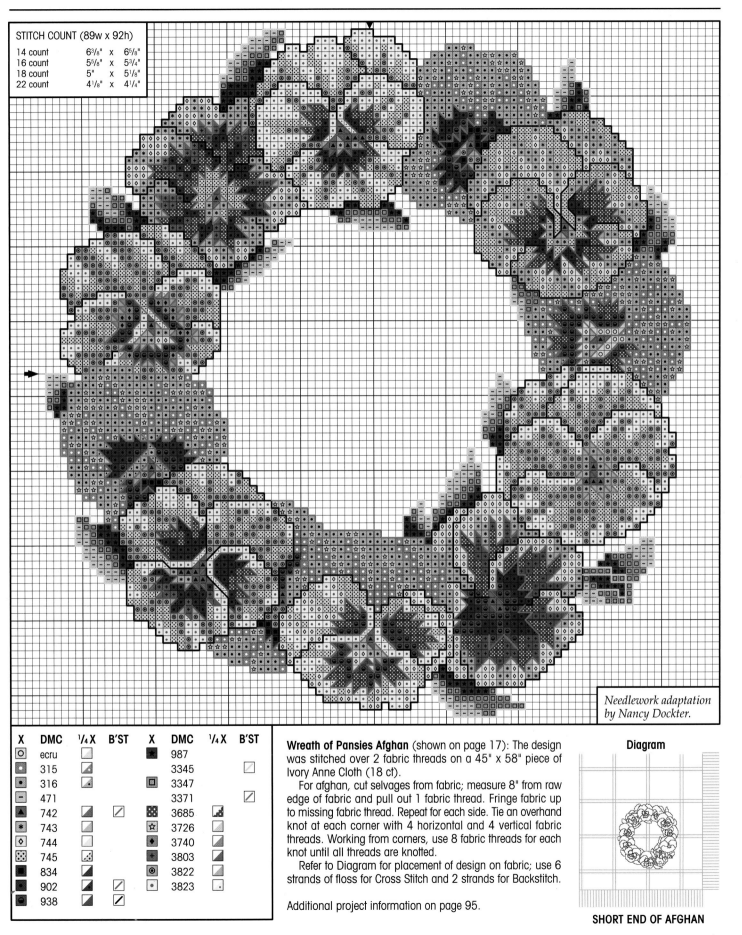

STITCH COUNT (89w x 92h)

14 count	6³⁄₈"	x	6⁵⁄₈"
16 count	5⁵⁄₈"	x	5³⁄₄"
18 count	5"	x	5¹⁄₈"
22 count	4¹⁄₈"	x	4¹⁄₄"

Needlework adaptation by Nancy Dockter.

Wreath of Pansies Afghan (shown on page 17): The design was stitched over 2 fabric threads on a 45" x 58" piece of Ivory Anne Cloth (18 ct).

For afghan, cut selvages from fabric; measure 8" from raw edge of fabric and pull out 1 fabric thread. Fringe fabric up to missing fabric thread. Repeat for each side. Tie an overhand knot at each corner with 4 horizontal and 4 vertical fabric threads. Working from corners, use 8 fabric threads for each knot until all threads are knotted.

Refer to Diagram for placement of design on fabric; use 6 strands of floss for Cross Stitch and 2 strands for Backstitch.

Additional project information on page 95.

Diagram

SHORT END OF AFGHAN

63

PICTUResQUE pANsies

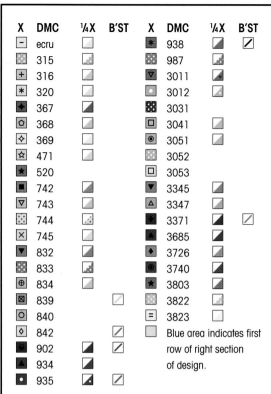

X	DMC	¼X	B'ST	X	DMC	¼X	B'ST
-	ecru			✱	938		
	315				987		
+	316			▽	3011		
✻	320				3012		
◆	367			✿	3031		
⬠	368			□	3041		
◇	369			◉	3051		
☆	471				3052		
★	520			□	3053		
■	742				3345		
▽	743			△	3347		
	744				3371		
✕	745				3685		
▼	832			◆	3726		
	833			◉	3740		
⊕	834			★	3803		
⊠	839				3822		
○	840			=	3823		
◇	842				Blue area indicates first		
◼	902				row of right section		
▲	934				of design.		
◗	935						

STITCH COUNT (145w x 109h)

14 count	10³/₈"	x	7⁷/₈"	
16 count	9¹/₈"	x	6⁷/₈"	
18 count	8¹/₈"	x	6¹/₈"	
22 count	6⁵/₈"	x	5"	

Pansies in Profusion in Frame (shown on pages 14-15): The design was stitched over 2 fabric threads on a 17" x 15" piece of Antique White Belfast Linen (32 ct). Two strands of floss were used for Cross Stitch and 1 strand for Backstitch. It was custom framed.

Pansy Pair Sachet Bag (shown on page 16): A portion of the design (refer to photo) was stitched over 2 fabric threads on an 8" x 12" piece of Cream Belfast Linen (32 ct). Two strands of floss were used for Cross Stitch and 1 strand for Backstitch.

For sachet bag, you will need a 4¹/₂" x 7¹/₂" piece of Belfast Linen for backing, 15" length of 1"w flat lace, 21" length of ¹/₄"w ribbon, polyester fiberfill, and scented oil.

Trim stitched piece to measure 4¹/₂" x 7¹/₂", allowing 1¹/₄" margins at sides, a 1¹/₂" margin at bottom, and a 3¹/₂" margin at top of design.

Matching right sides and leaving top edge open, use a ¹/₂" seam allowance to sew stitched piece and backing fabric together; trim seam allowances diagonally at corners. Turn top edge of bag ¹/₄" to wrong side and press; turn ¹/₄" to wrong side again and hem. Press short edges of lace ¹/₂" to wrong side and machine baste close to straight edge; gather lace to fit top of bag. Blind stitch gathered edge of lace to wrong side of top edge of bag; turn bag right side out. Stuff bag with polyester fiberfill. Place a few drops of scented oil on a small amount of fiberfill and insert in bag. Tie ribbon in a bow around bag; trim ends as desired.

Needlework adaptation by Nancy Dockter.

IN THE ORCHARD

X	DMC	½ X	B'ST
▽	355		
☆	402		
	436	▲	
	437	☒	
✚	632		
⊙	726		
▼	730		
◖	733		
−	734		
✔ *	734 &		
	3046		
	738	⊙	
◆	743		
2	744		
✛	745		
⊙	890		
★ *	890 &		
	935		
▲	921		
◉	922		
•	935		◢
■ *	935 &		
	898		
=	937		
✳	3011		
H *	3011 &		
	3346		
▼	3046		
◇	3047		◢
☐	3346	◆	
☒	3347		
◼	3777		

* For linen, use 2 strands of first floss color listed and 1 strand of second floss color listed. For afghan, use 3 strands of each floss color listed.

STITCH COUNT (72w x 119h)

14 count	5¼"	x 8½"
16 count	4½"	x 7½"
18 count	4"	x 6⅝"
22 count	3⅜"	x 5½"

Peaches & Plums in Frames (shown on pages 18 and 20): Each design was stitched over 2 fabric threads on a 13" x 17" piece of Tea-Dyed Irish Linen (28 ct). Three strands of floss were used for Cross Stitch and 1 strand for Half Cross Stitch and Backstitch. They were custom framed.

Peaches Afghan (shown on page 19): A portion of the design (refer to photo) was stitched over 2 fabric threads on a 45" x 58" piece of Ivory Anne Cloth (18 ct).

For afghan, cut selvages from fabric; measure 5½" from raw edge of fabric and pull out 1 fabric thread. Repeat for each side. Tie an overhand knot at each corner with 4 horizontal and 4 vertical fabric threads. Working from corners, use 8 fabric threads for each knot until all threads are knotted.

Refer to Diagram (page 67) for placement of design on fabric; use 6 strands of floss for Cross Stitch and 2 strands for Backstitch.

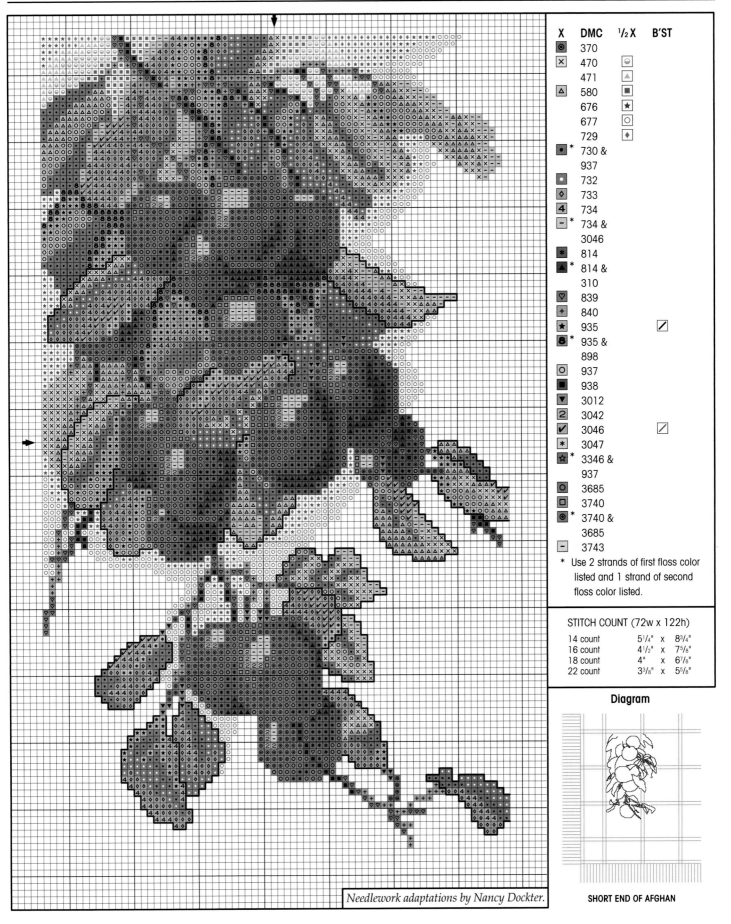

X	DMC	½ X	B'ST
⊙	370		
☒	470	⊖	
	471	△	
△	580	■	
	676	★	
	677	○	
	729	◆	
■ *	730 &		
	937		
⊡	732		
◇	733		
4	734		
− *	734 &		
	3046		
✳	814		
▲ *	814 &		
	310		
♡	839		
+	840		
★	935		◿
8 *	935 &		
	898		
○	937		
■	938		
▼	3012		
2	3042		
✔	3046		◿
✳	3047		
☆ *	3346 &		
	937		
◉	3685		
▢	3740		
◉ *	3740 &		
	3685		
−	3743		

* Use 2 strands of first floss color
listed and 1 strand of second
floss color listed.

STITCH COUNT (72w x 122h)

14 count	5¼"	x	8¾"
16 count	4½"	x	7⅝"
18 count	4"	x	6⅞"
22 count	3⅜"	x	5⅝"

Diagram

SHORT END OF AFGHAN

Needlework adaptations by Nancy Dockter.

67

IN THE ORCHARD

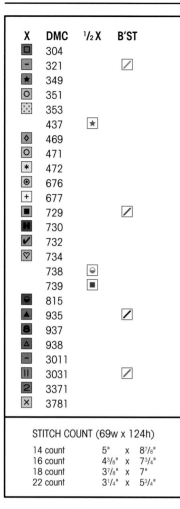

X	DMC	½X	B'ST
▣	304		
-	321		╱
★	349		
○	351		
⠿	353		
	437	★	
◆	469		
○	471		
✳	472		
◉	676		
+	677		
■	729		╱
ℍ	730		
✔	732		
▽	734		
	738	◉	
	739	■	
⬛	815		
▲	935		╱
8	937		
◭	938		
⊟	3011		
‖	3031		╱
2	3371		
✕	3781		

STITCH COUNT (69w x 124h)

14 count	5"	x	8⅞"
16 count	4⅜"	x	7¾"
18 count	3⅞"	x	7"
22 count	3¼"	x	5¾"

Apples and Pears in Frames (shown on page 21): Each design was stitched over 2 fabric threads on a 13" x 17" piece of Tea-Dyed Irish Linen (28 ct). Three strands of floss were used for Cross Stitch and 1 strand for Half Cross Stitch and Backstitch. They were custom framed.

Needlework adaptations by Nancy Dockter and Grace Domagala-Zobkow.

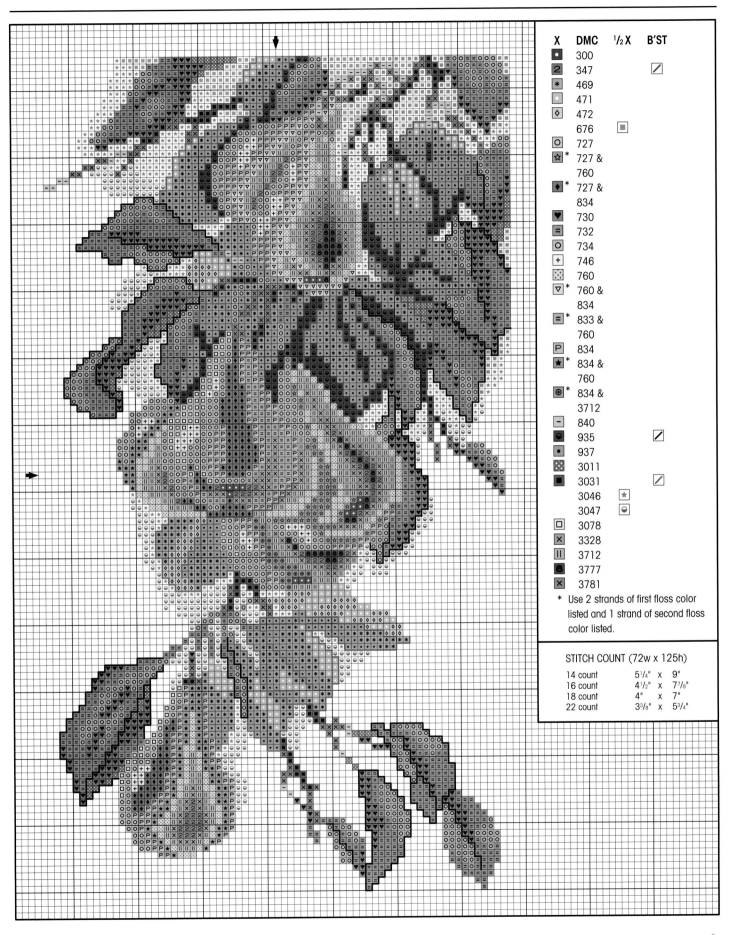

X	DMC	½X	B'ST
■	300		
2	347		╱
✳	469		
●	471		
◇	472		
	676	▦	
O	727		
☆*	727 &		
	760		
◆*	727 &		
	834		
♥	730		
▦	732		
⊙	734		
+	746		
▦	760		
▽*	760 &		
	834		
▦*	833 &		
	760		
P	834		
★*	834 &		
	760		
◉*	834 &		
	3712		
−	840		
●	935		╱
•	937		
▦	3011		
■	3031		╱
	3046	★	
	3047	⊖	
▢	3078		
✕	3328		
‖	3712		
8	3777		
✕	3781		

* Use 2 strands of first floss color
  listed and 1 strand of second floss
  color listed.

STITCH COUNT (72w x 125h)

14 count	5¼"	x	9"
16 count	4½"	x	7⅞"
18 count	4"	x	7"
22 count	3⅜"	x	5¾"

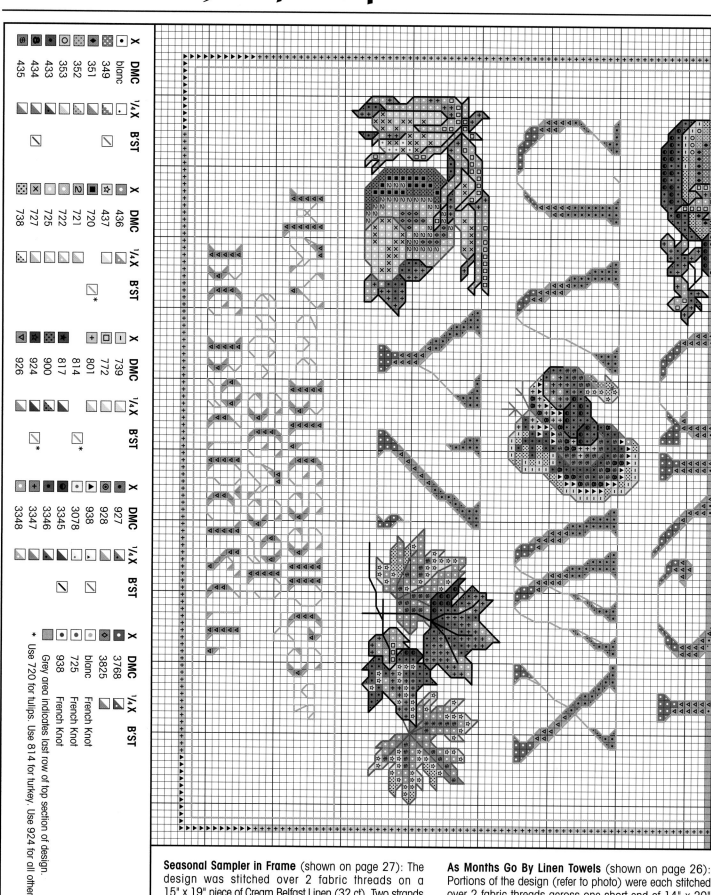

X	DMC	1/4X	B'ST
	blanc		
	349		
	351		
	352		
	353		
	433		
	434		
	435		

X	DMC	1/4X	B'ST
	436		
	437		
	720		*
	721		
	722		
	725		
	727		
	738		

X	DMC	1/4X	B'ST
	739		
	772		*
	801		
	814		
	817		
	900		
	924		
	926		

X	DMC	1/4X	B'ST
	927		
	928		
	938		
	3078		
	3345		
	3346		
	3347		
	3348		

X	DMC	1/4X	B'ST
	3768		
	3825		
	blanc	French Knot	
	725	French Knot	
	938	French Knot	

* Use 720 for tulips. Use 814 for turkey. Use 924 for all other.

Seasonal Sampler in Frame (shown on page 27): The design was stitched over 2 fabric threads on a 15" x 19" piece of Cream Belfast Linen (32 ct). Two strands of floss were used for Cross Stitch and 1 strand for Backstitch and French Knots. It was custom framed.

As Months Go By Linen Towels (shown on page 26): Portions of the design (refer to photo) were each stitched over 2 fabric threads across one short end of 14" x 20" piece of Cream Belfast Linen (32 ct). For monogrammed towels, leave 2 squares between letters and 6 squares

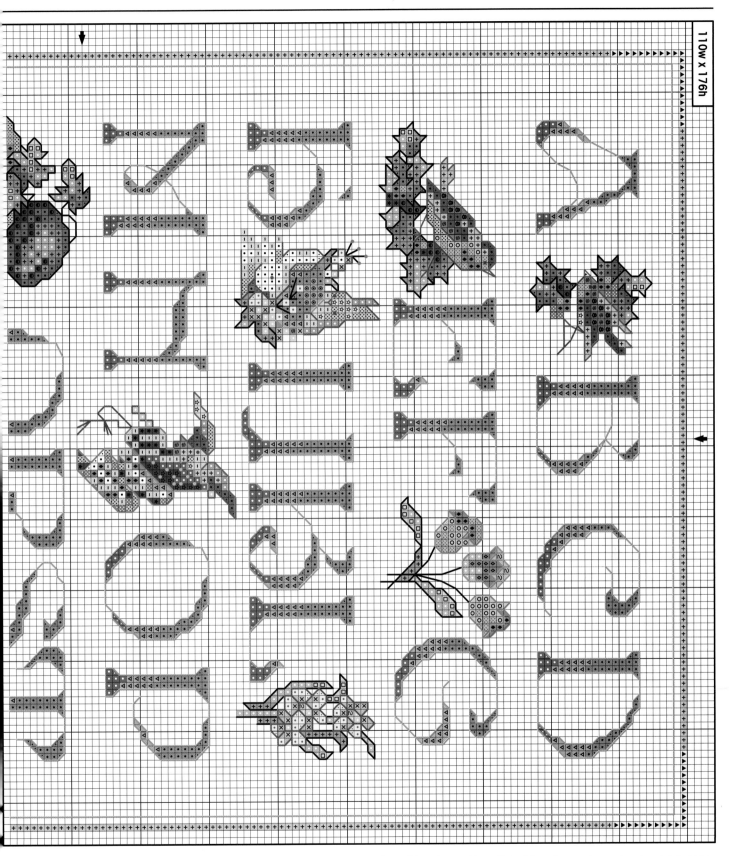

between letters and motifs. For "May the Blessings" towel, leave 3 squares between verse and motifs. Center designs horizontally with bottom of designs 1½" from short edge. Two strands of floss were used for Cross Stitch and 1 strand for Backstitch and French Knots.

For towel, machine stitch across each short edge of fabric ½" from raw edges. Fringe to machine-stitched line. On one long edge, turn fabric ¼" to wrong side and press; turn ¼" to wrong side again and hem. Repeat for remaining long edge.

Design by Donna Vermillion Giampa.

as months go by

X	DMC	¼ X	½ X	B'ST
-	ecru	☐		
▣	223			
◉	341			
◆	347			◹
▲	500	◺		◹
◒	501	◺		
▢	502	◺		
=	503	☐		
▨	520			
▦	610	◪	■	◹
■	611	◺	◒	
▢	612	◺	＋	
◇	613	◺	▲	
♥	640	◺		◹
○	642	☐		
•	644	◪		
2	725			
★	726			
＋	727			
▽	745			
	747		○	
☆	760	◺		
‖	761			
	781			◹
◉	783			
＊	822	◺		
▦	3328			
H	3345	◺		
$	3346	◺	▽	
•	3347	◪	★	
✕	3348			
	3371	◤		◹
▣	3712	◺		
✔	3713			
△	3721			
	3761		★	

STITCH COUNT (75w x 117h)

14 count	5³/₈"	x	8³/₈"	
16 count	4³/₄"	x	7³/₈"	
18 count	4¹/₄"	x	6¹/₂"	
22 count	3¹/₂"	x	5³/₈"	

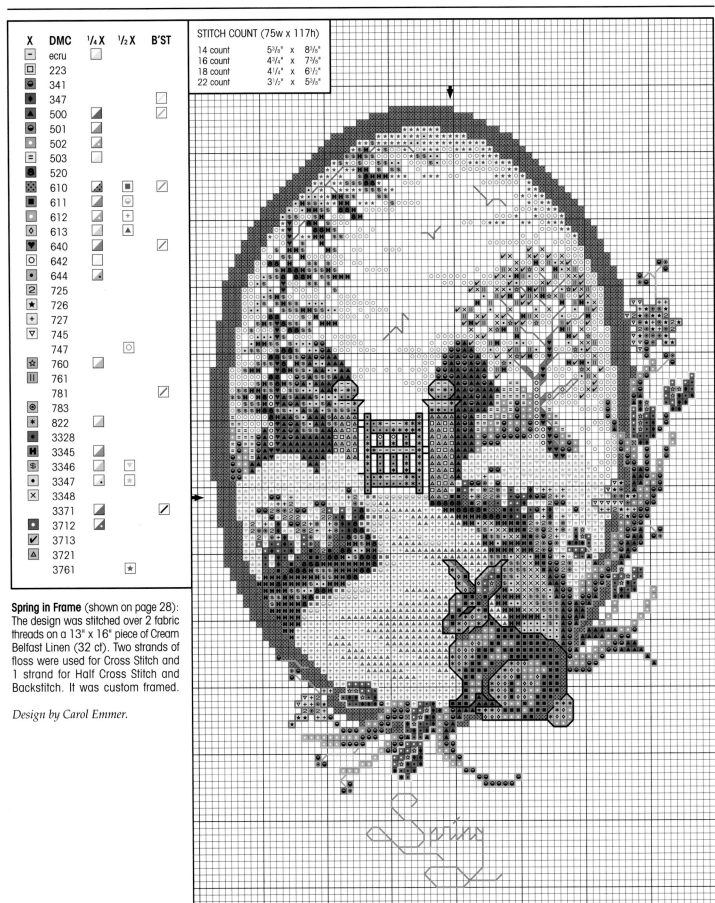

Spring in Frame (shown on page 28): The design was stitched over 2 fabric threads on a 13" x 16" piece of Cream Belfast Linen (32 ct). Two strands of floss were used for Cross Stitch and 1 strand for Half Cross Stitch and Backstitch. It was custom framed.

Design by Carol Emmer.

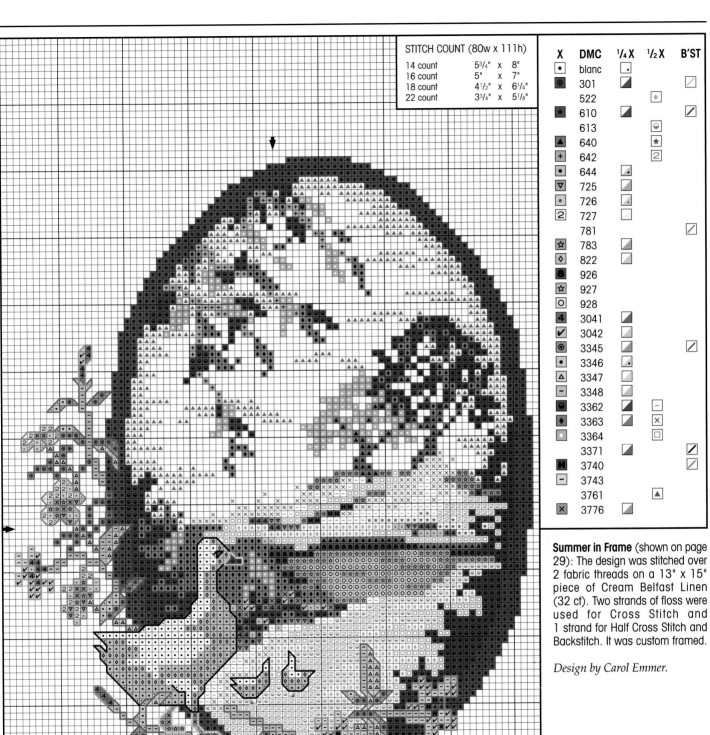

STITCH COUNT (80w x 111h)

14 count	5¾"	x	8"
16 count	5"	x	7"
18 count	4½"	x	6¼"
22 count	3¾"	x	5⅛"

X	DMC	¼ X	½ X	B'ST
•	blanc	•		
◉	301	◣		◤
	522		◆	
✻	610	◣		◤
	613		◙	
▲	640		★	
+	642		2	
•	644	•		
▽	725	◣		
•	726		•	
2	727	□		
	781			◤
☆	783	◣		
◇	822	◣		
⑧	926			
☆	927			
○	928			
4	3041	◣		
✔	3042	◣		
◉	3345	◣		◤
•	3346	•		
△	3347	◣		
−	3348	◣		
◙	3362	◣	−	
◆	3363	◣	✕	
◙	3364		□	
	3371	◣		◤
H	3740	◣		◤
−	3743			
	3761		▲	
✕	3776	◣		

Summer in Frame (shown on page 29): The design was stitched over 2 fabric threads on a 13" x 15" piece of Cream Belfast Linen (32 ct). Two strands of floss were used for Cross Stitch and 1 strand for Half Cross Stitch and Backstitch. It was custom framed.

Design by Carol Emmer.

AS MONTHS GO BY

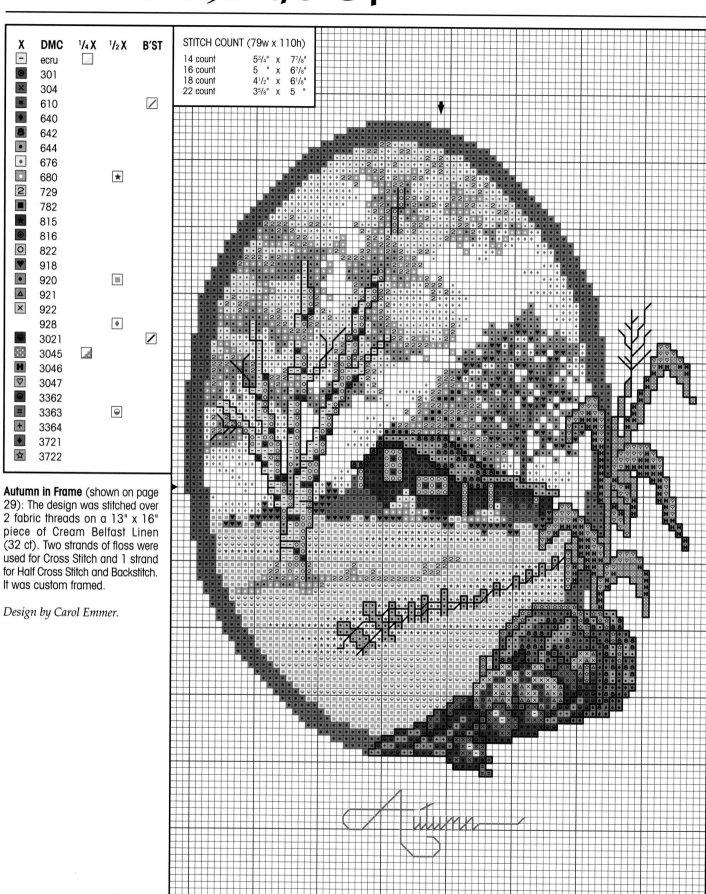

X	DMC	¼ X	½ X	B'ST
−	ecru	☐		
◉	301			
✕	304			╱
✳	610			╱
◆	640			
⦾	642			
•	644			
·	676			
○	680		★	
2	729			
■	782			
★	815			
◉	816			
○	822			
♥	918			
●	920		▪	
△	921			
✕	922			
	928		◆	
▣	3021			╱
▦	3045	◩		
H	3046			
♡	3047			
◖	3362			
⊟	3363		◖	
+	3364			
◆	3721			
☆	3722			

STITCH COUNT (79w x 110h)

14 count	5¾"	x	7⅞"	
16 count	5 "	x	6⅞"	
18 count	4½"	x	6⅛"	
22 count	3⅝"	x	5 "	

Autumn in Frame (shown on page 29): The design was stitched over 2 fabric threads on a 13" x 16" piece of Cream Belfast Linen (32 ct). Two strands of floss were used for Cross Stitch and 1 strand for Half Cross Stitch and Backstitch. It was custom framed.

Design by Carol Emmer.

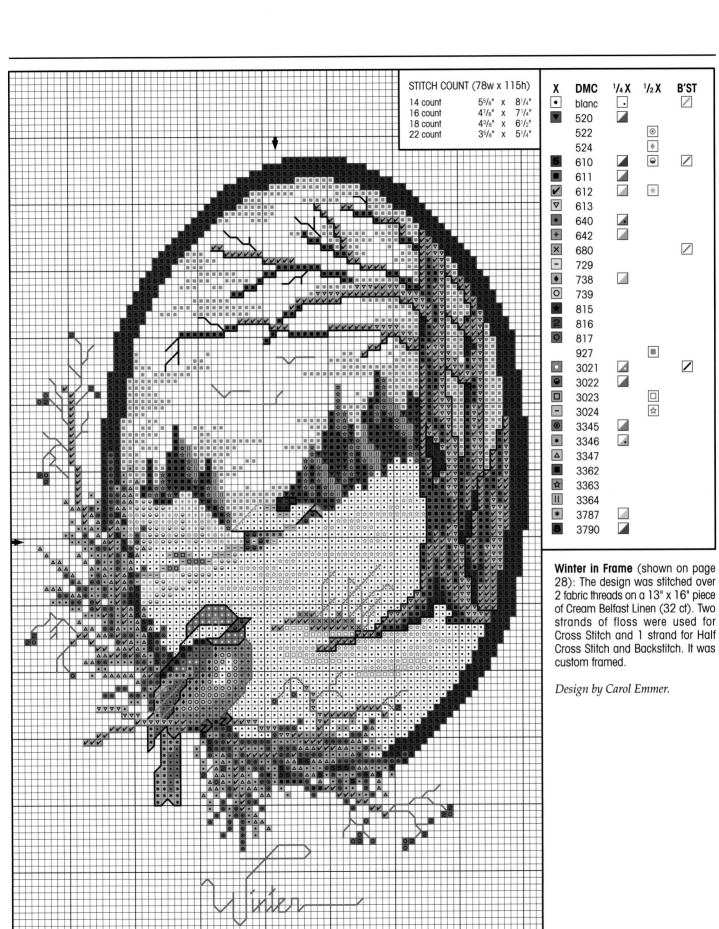

STITCH COUNT (78w x 115h)

14 count	5⅝"	x 8¼"
16 count	4⅞"	x 7¼"
18 count	4⅜"	x 6½"
22 count	3⅝"	x 5¼"

X	DMC	¼ X	½ X	B'ST
•	blanc	•		╱
▼	520	◢		
	522		◉	
	524		◆	
5	610	◣	◉	╱
■	611	◢		
✔	612	◢	★	
▽	613			
•	640	◢		
+	642	◢		
✕	680			╱
–	729			
◆	738	◢		
○	739			
★	815			
2	816			
◎	817			
	927		■	
◉	3021	◢		╱
◒	3022	◢		
□	3023		□	
–	3024		☆	
◉	3345	◢		
•	3346	◢		
△	3347			
■	3362			
☆	3363			
‖	3364			
✳	3787	◢		
8	3790	◢		

Winter in Frame (shown on page 28): The design was stitched over 2 fabric threads on a 13" x 16" piece of Cream Belfast Linen (32 ct). Two strands of floss were used for Cross Stitch and 1 strand for Half Cross Stitch and Backstitch. It was custom framed.

Design by Carol Emmer.

GOLDEN SUMMER DAYS

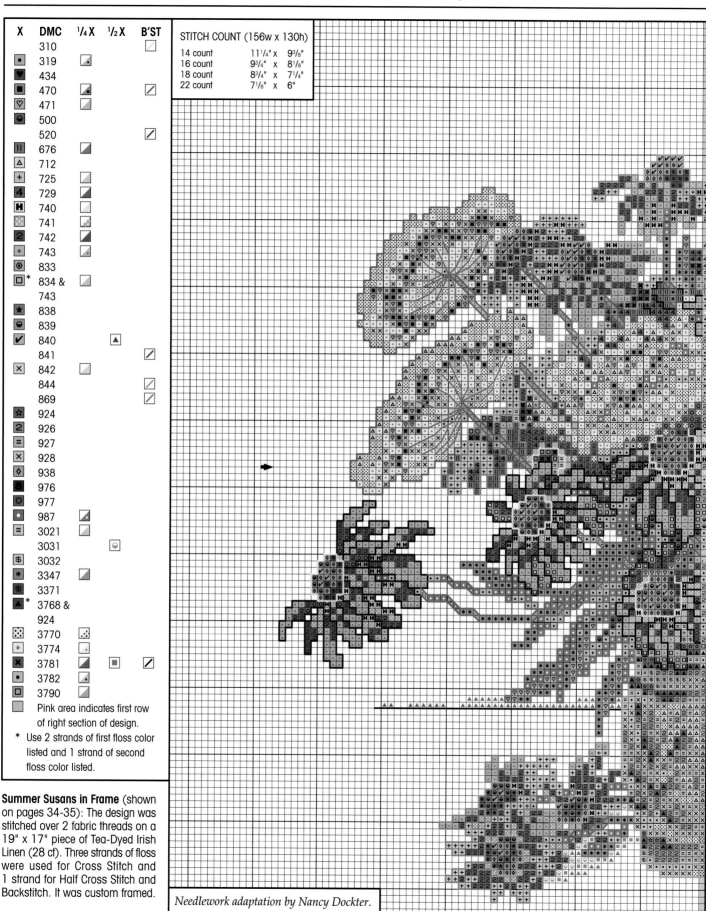

X	DMC	1/4 X	1/2 X	B'ST
	310			□
•	319	◢		
♥	434			
■	470	◢		◿
♡	471	◢		
◒	500			
	520			◿
‖	676	◢		
△	712			
+	725	◢		
4	729	◢		
H	740	◢		
▨	741	◢		
2	742	◢		
⊡	743	◢		
◉	833			
□ *	834 &	◢		
	743			
★	838			
◒	839			
✔	840		▲	
	841			◿
✕	842	◢		
	844			◿
	869			◿
☆	924			
2	926			
=	927			
✕	928			
◇	938			
■	976			
◎	977			
◈	987	◢		
=	3021	◢		
	3031		◒	
$	3032			
✳	3347	◢		
▣	3371			
▲ *	3768 &			
	924			
⦂⦂	3770	⦂		
◦	3774	◦		
✕	3781	◢	■	◿
•	3782	◦		
▢	3790	◢		
▨		Pink area indicates first row		
		of right section of design.		

STITCH COUNT (156w x 130h)

14 count	11 1/4" x	9 3/8"
16 count	9 3/4" x	8 1/8"
18 count	8 3/4" x	7 1/4"
22 count	7 1/8" x	6"

* Use 2 strands of first floss color
listed and 1 strand of second
floss color listed.

Summer Susans in Frame (shown
on pages 34-35): The design was
stitched over 2 fabric threads on a
19" x 17" piece of Tea-Dyed Irish
Linen (28 ct). Three strands of floss
were used for Cross Stitch and
1 strand for Half Cross Stitch and
Backstitch. It was custom framed.

Needlework adaptation by Nancy Dockter.

GOLDEN SUMMER DAYS

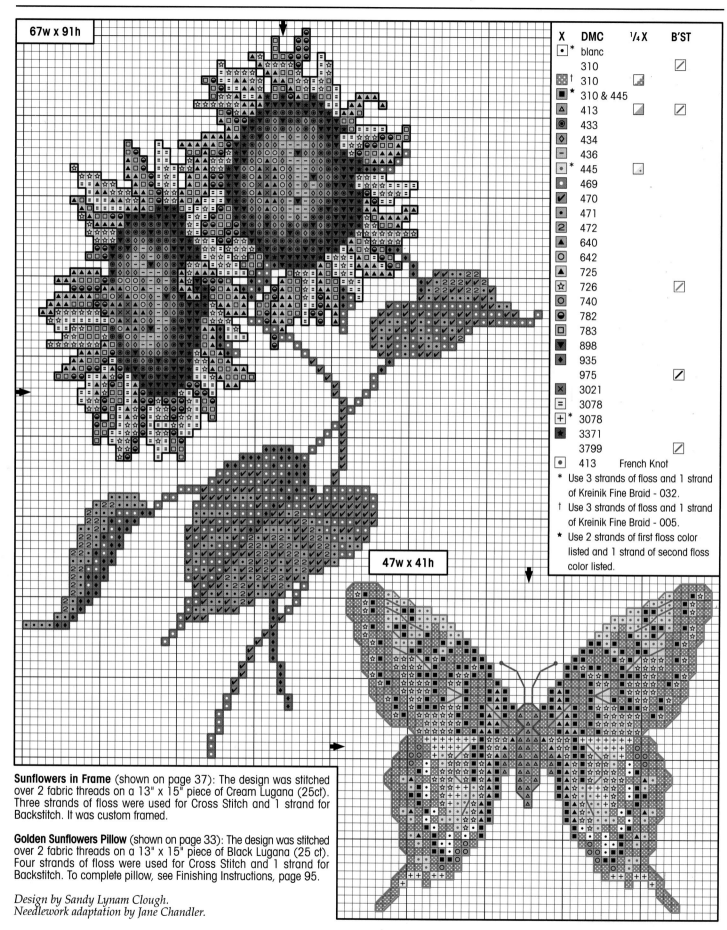

67w x 91h

47w x 41h

X	DMC	¼ X	B'ST
•*	blanc		
	310		/
†	310	▨	
■*	310 & 445		
▲	413	◪	/
◉	433		
◇	434		
-	436		
•*	445	▫	
▨	469		
☑	470		
•	471		
2	472		
▲	640		
◎	642		
▲	725		
☆	726		/
◯	740		
◖	782		
▢	783		
▼	898		
◆	935		
	975		/
✕	3021		
=	3078		
+*	3078		
★	3371		
	3799		/
◉	413	French Knot	

* Use 3 strands of floss and 1 strand
of Kreinik Fine Braid - 032.

† Use 3 strands of floss and 1 strand
of Kreinik Fine Braid - 005.

* Use 2 strands of first floss color
listed and 1 strand of second floss
color listed.

Sunflowers in Frame (shown on page 37): The design was stitched over 2 fabric threads on a 13" x 15" piece of Cream Lugana (25ct). Three strands of floss were used for Cross Stitch and 1 strand for Backstitch. It was custom framed.

Golden Sunflowers Pillow (shown on page 33): The design was stitched over 2 fabric threads on a 13" x 15" piece of Black Lugana (25 ct). Four strands of floss were used for Cross Stitch and 1 strand for Backstitch. To complete pillow, see Finishing Instructions, page 95.

Design by Sandy Lynam Clough.
Needlework adaptation by Jane Chandler.

68w x 104h

Needlework adaptation by Carol Emmer.

X	DMC	¼X	B'ST
▲	301		
■	322		
●	334	◪	
	336		◹
+	402		
▢	434		
◆	436		
◖	437		
◕	470		
▨	471		
❙❙❙	472		
O	597		
▧	610		
●	611		
▤	612		
●	712	◪	◹
◇	725		
O	726	◪	
+	727	▢	
▦	738		
−	775		
H	780		
✔	782		
−	783		
☆	801		
	898		◹
	935		◹
✕	3325		
◧	3371	◪	◹*
2	3755		
$	3776		
▼	3810		

* For antennae, work in long stitches.

Butterfly in Frame (shown on page 32, chart on page 78): The design was stitched over 2 fabric threads on a 12" square of Cream Lugana (25 ct). Three strands of floss were used for Cross Stitch and 1 strand for Backstitch and French Knots, unless otherwise noted in the color key. It was custom framed.

Butterfly Box (shown on page 37, chart on page 78): The design was stitched over 2 fabric threads on a 12" square of Black Lugana (25 ct). Three strands of floss were used for Cross Stitch and 1 strand for Backstitch and French Knots, unless otherwise noted in the color key. It was inserted in the lid of a purchased box (5" square opening).

Winged Beauties in Frame (shown on page 36): The design was stitched over 2 fabric threads on a 13" x 16" piece of Cream Lugana (25 ct). Three strands of floss were used for Cross Stitch and 1 strand for Backstitch. It was custom framed.

Design by Donna Vermillion Giampa.

ROSE GARDEN TEA

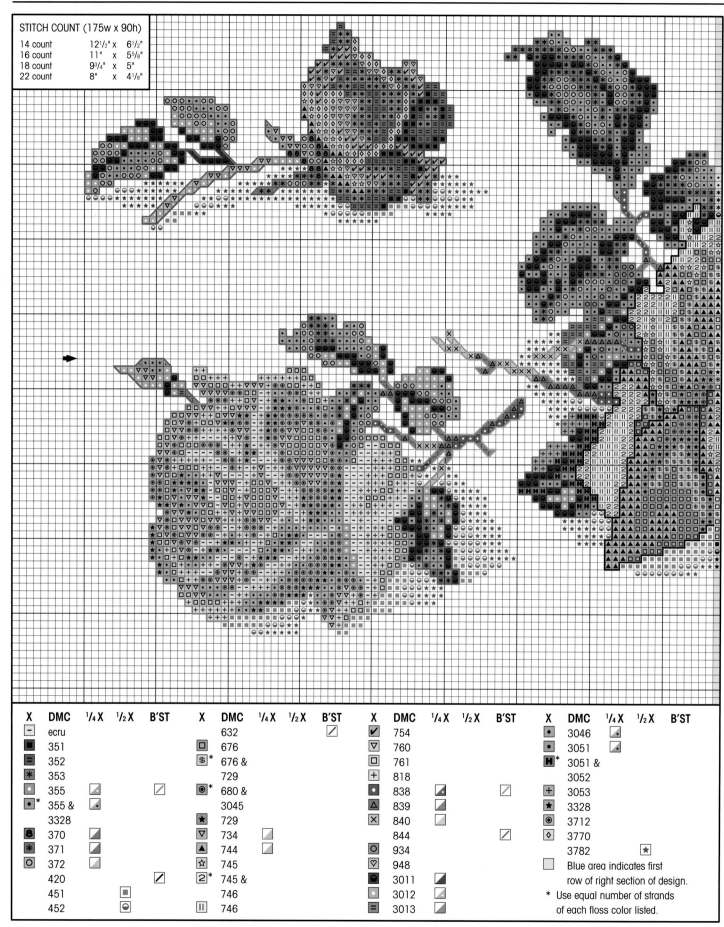

STITCH COUNT (175w x 90h)

14 count	12½"	x	6½"
16 count	11"	x	5⅝"
18 count	9¾"	x	5"
22 count	8"	x	4⅛"

X	DMC	¼X	½X	B'ST	X	DMC	¼X	½X	B'ST	X	DMC	¼X	½X	B'ST	X	DMC	¼X	½X	B'ST
−	ecru					632			◢	✔	754				•	3046	◿		
■	351				□	676				▽	760				•	3051	◿		
≡	352				$ *	676 &				□	761				H *	3051 &			
✳	353					729				+	818					3052			
✿	355	◿		◿	◉ *	680 &				◙	838	◢		◿	+	3053			
• *	355 &	◢				3045				▲	839	◢			★	3328			
	3328				★	729				✕	840	◢			◉	3712			
8	370	◢			▽	734		◿			844		◿		◇	3770			
✳	371	◢			▲	744				O	934					3782		★	
O	372	◢			☆	745				▽	948								
	420			◿	2 *	745 &				◙	3011	◢			☐	Blue area indicates first			
	451		■			746				◙	3012	◢				row of right section of design.			
	452		◙	‖		746				◙	3013	◿				* Use equal number of strands of each floss color listed.			

Roses for Thee in Frame (shown on pages 40-41): The design was stitched over 2 fabric threads on a 19" x 14" piece of Cream Belfast Linen (32 ct). Two strands of floss were used for Cross Stitch and 1 strand for Half Cross Stitch and Backstitch. It was custom framed.

Roses for Thee Afghan (shown on page 39): A portion of the design (refer to photo) was stitched over 2 fabric threads on a 45" x 58" piece of Ivory All-Cotton Anne Cloth (18 ct).

For afghan, cut selvages from fabric; measure 5¹/₂" from raw edge of fabric and pull out one fabric thread. Fringe fabric up to missing thread. Repeat for each side. Tie an overhand knot at each corner with 4 horizontal and 4 vertical fabric threads. Working from corners, use 8 fabric threads for each knot until all threads are knotted.

Refer to Diagram for placement of design on fabric; use 6 strands of floss for Cross Stitch and 2 strands for Half Cross Stitch and Backstitch.

Diagram

SHORT END OF AFGHAN

Needlework adaptation by Nancy Dockter.

ROSE GARDEN TEA

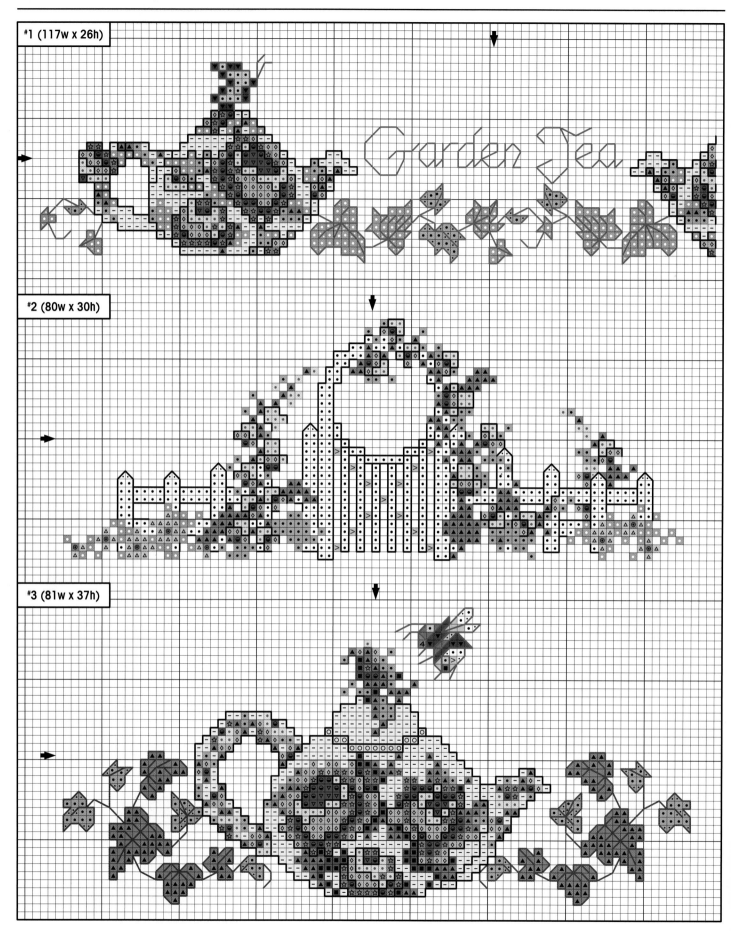

#1 (117w x 26h)

#2 (80w x 30h)

#3 (81w x 37h)

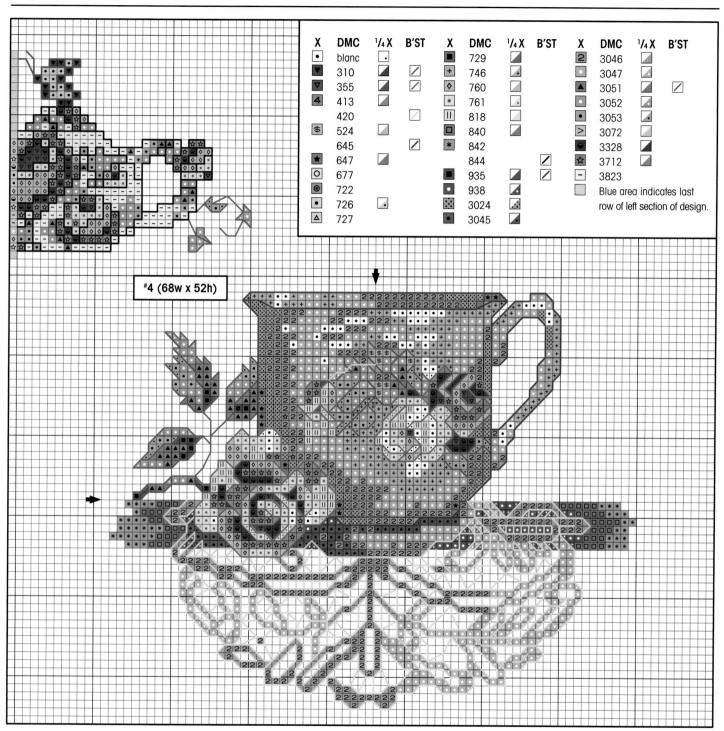

X	DMC	¼X	B'ST	X	DMC	¼X	B'ST	X	DMC	¼X	B'ST
•	blanc	•		■	729	◩		2	3046	◩	
▼	310	◩	◹	+	746	◩	+	○	3047	◩	◹
▽	355	◩	◹	◇	760	◩		▲	3051	◩	◹
4	413	◩		•	761	•		●	3052	◩	
	420		◹	‖	818			•	3053	◪	
$	524	◩		▢	840	◩		>	3072	◩	
	645		◹	✳	842			◓	3328	◩	
★	647	◩			844		◹	☆	3712	◩	
○	677			■	935		◹	−	3823		
⊙	722			•	938	◩		▨	Blue area indicates last		
•	726	◪		▦	3024	◪			row of left section of design.		
△	727			•	3045	◩					

#4 (68w x 52h)

Rose Garden Tea Towels (shown on page 42): Designs #1, #2, and #3 were each stitched over 2 fabric threads across one short end of a 13½" x 19" piece of Cream Belfast Linen (32 ct). Center each design horizontally with bottom of design 1¾" from short edge. Two strands of floss were used for Cross Stitch and 1 strand for Backstitch.

For each towel, you will need a 13½" length of 1"w flat lace.

On cross-stitched end, match straight edge of lace to raw edge of fabric and use a ¼" seam allowance to sew lace to right side of fabric. Using a zigzag stitch to prevent fraying, sew close to seam; trim close to zigzag stitch. Press seam allowance to wrong side of towel. For remaining raw edges, turn fabric ¼" to wrong side and press; turn ¼" to wrong side again and hem.

Designs by Diane Brakefield.

Rose Teacup in Frame (shown on page 38): Design #4 was stitched over 2 fabric threads on a 12" x 11" piece of Cream Belfast Linen (32 ct). Two strands of floss were used for Cross Stitch and 1 strand for Backstitch. It was custom framed.

Design by Sandy Lynam Clough.
Needlework adaptation by Donna Vermillion Giampa.

ROSE GARDEN TEA

STITCH COUNT (94w x 122h)

14 count	6³/₄"	x	8³/₄"
16 count	5⁷/₈"	x	7⁵/₈"
18 count	5¹/₄"	x	6⁷/₈"
22 count	4³/₈"	x	5⁵/₈"

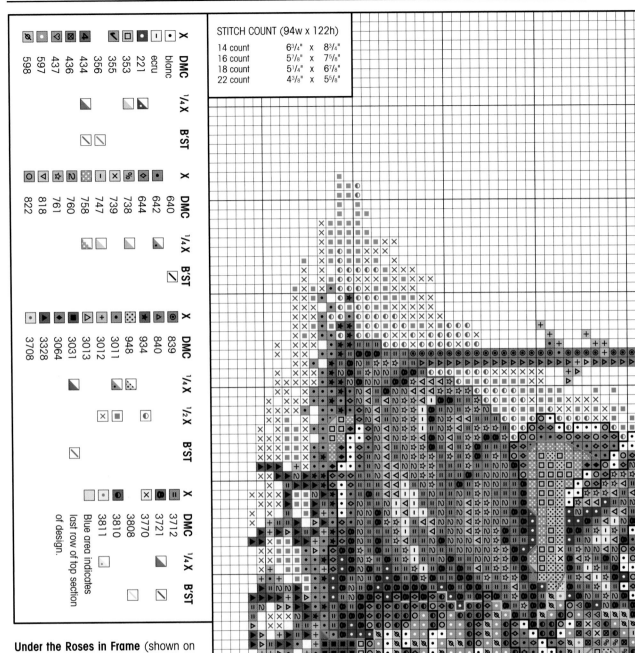

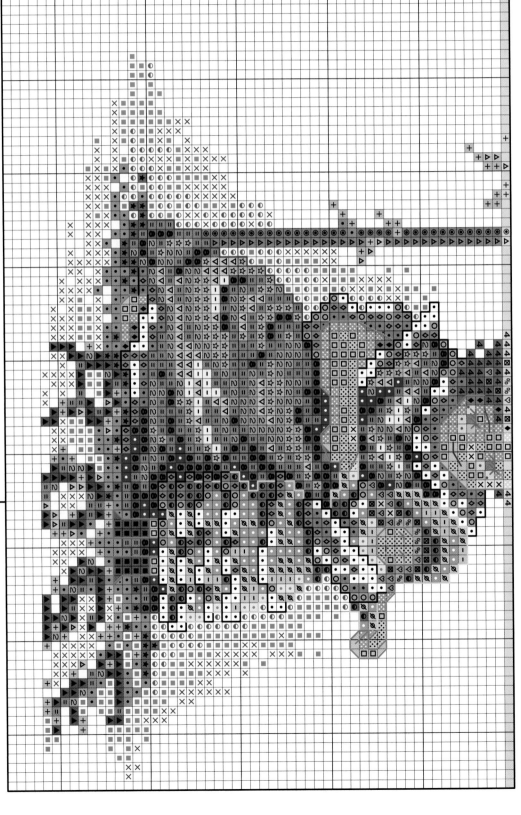

Under the Roses in Frame (shown on page 43): The design was stitched over 2 fabric threads on a 15" x 17" piece of Cream Cashel Linen® (28 ct). Three strands of floss were used for Cross Stitch and 1 strand for Half Cross Stitch and Backstitch. It was custom framed.

Needlework adaptation by Carol Emmer.

earth speaks in flowers

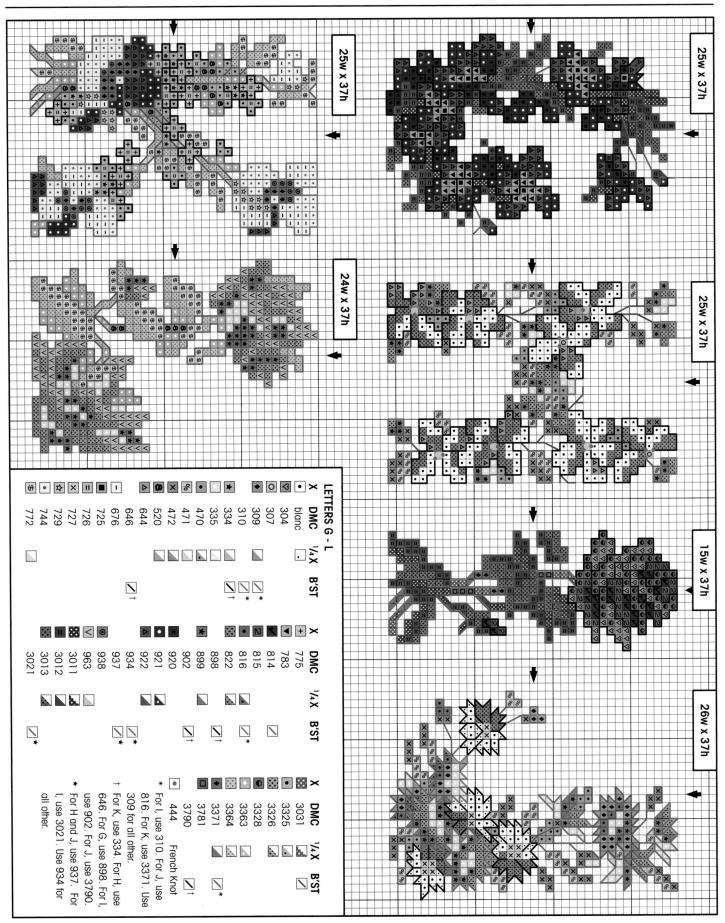

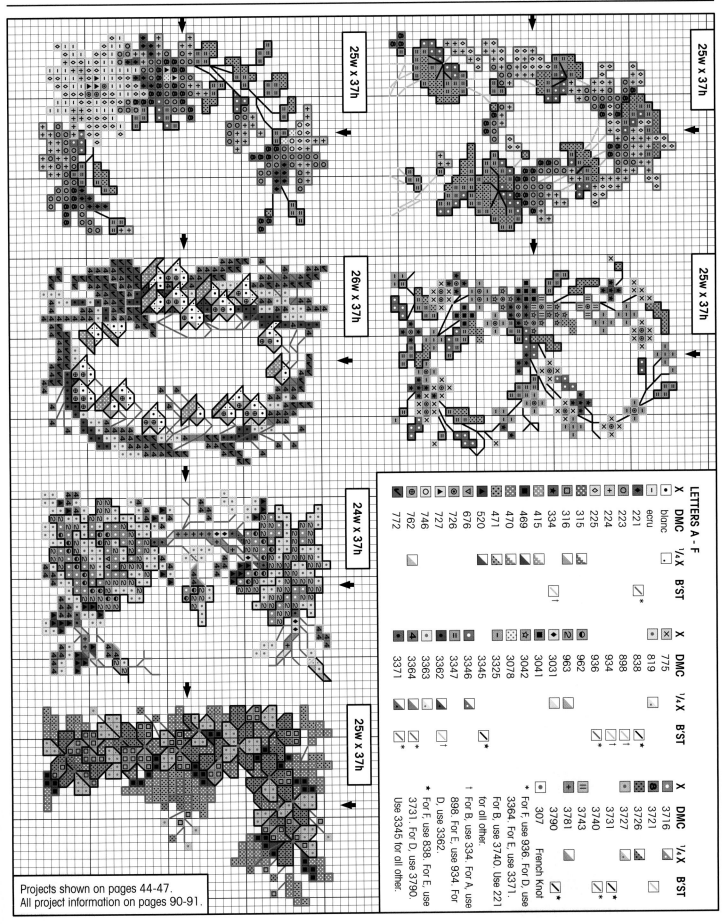

25w x 37h

25w x 37h

25w x 37h

26w x 37h

25w x 37h

24w x 37h

25w x 37h

LETTERS A - F

X		¼X	B'ST	DMC
◪	•	•	◪	blanc
⊕		◪	◪ *	ecru
○				221
▶				223
◉				224
◁				225
▼				315
■				316
▨			◪ †	334
▨				415
■				469
★				470
□				471
◇			◪	520
+				676
◉				726
◆				727
I				746
•		◪		762
				772

X		¼X	B'ST	DMC
•	×		◪	775
×		◪		819
			◪	838
■				898
◢		◪	◪ *	934
•				936
●				962
II			◪ †	963
○				3025
I			◪	3031
⊡				3041
☆				3042
■				3078
◆				3325
②			◪ *	3345
◐			◪ †	3346
				3347
				3362
			◪	3363
			◪	3364
			◪ *	3371

X		¼X	B'ST	DMC
•	•	◪	◪	307
+				3716
II				3721
•		◪	◪ *	3726
⊠		◪	◪ *	3727
•		◪	◪	3731
				3740
				3743
				3781
				3790

• 307 French Knot

* For F, use 936. For D, use 3364. For E, use 3371.

† For B, use 334. For A, use 3740. Use 221 for all other.

★ For B, use 898. For E, use 934. For D, use 3362.

◆ For F, use 838. For E, use 3731. For D, use 3790. Use 3345 for all other.

Projects shown on pages 44-47.
All project information on pages 90-91.

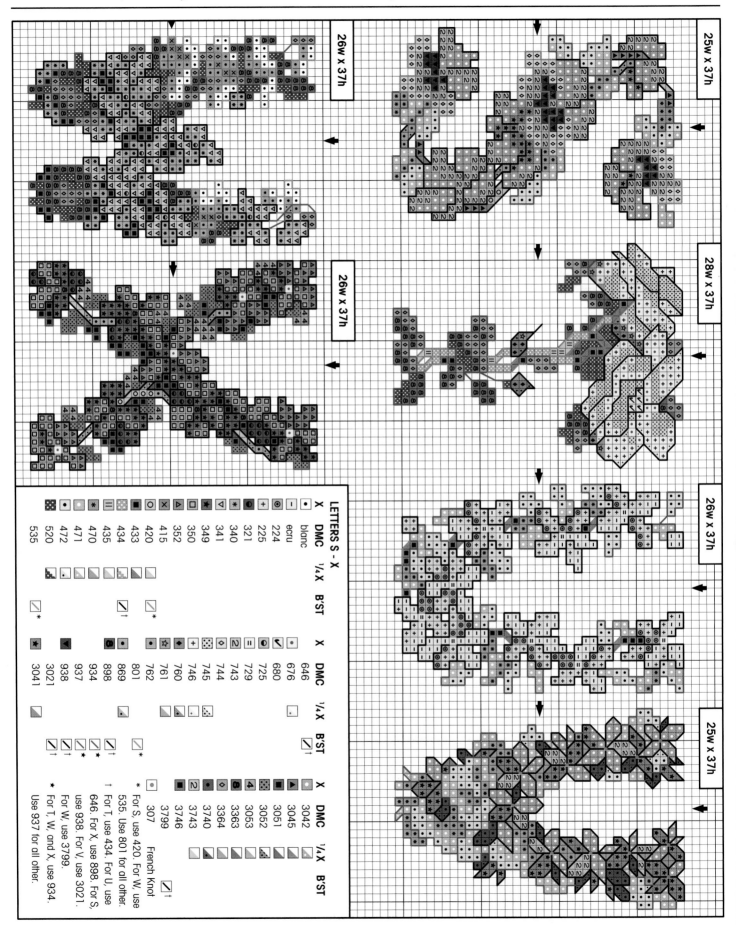

26w x 37h
25w x 37h
26w x 37h
28w x 37h
26w x 37h
25w x 37h

LETTERS S - X

X	DMC	¼X	B'ST
●	blanc		
○	ecru		
*	224		
=	225		
	321		
	340		
	341		
	349		
	350		
	352		
	415		
	420		*
	433		
	434		†
	435		
	470		
	471		*
	472		
	520		
	535		*

X	DMC	¼X	B'ST
	646		†
	676		
	680		
	725		
	729		
	743		
	744		
	745		
	746		
	760		
	761		*
	762		
	801		†
	869		
	898		†
	934		*
	937		*
	938		†
	3021		
	3041		

X	DMC	¼X	B'ST
	307		†
	3799		
	3746		
	3743		
	3740		
	3364		
	3363		
	3053		
	3052		
	3051		
	3045		
	3042		

French Knot

* For S, use 420. For W, use 535. Use 801 for all other.
† For T, use 434. For U, use 646. For X, use 898. For S, use 938. For V, use 3021. For W, use 3799. For T, W, and X, use 934. Use 937 for all other.

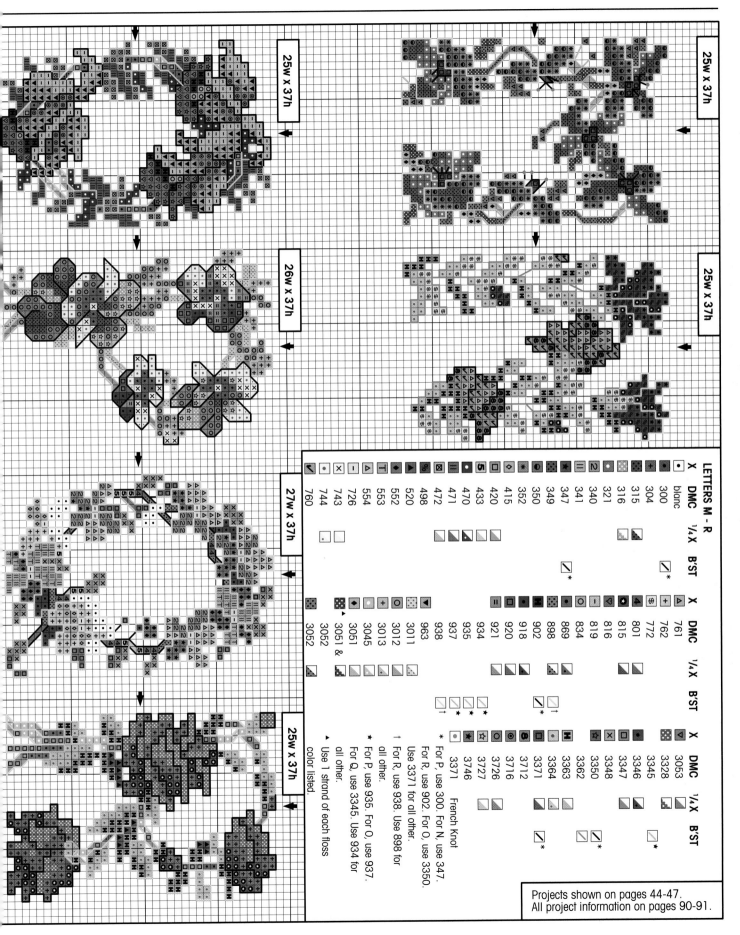

25w x 37h

25w x 37h

26w x 37h

25w x 37h

27w x 37h

25w x 37h

LETTERS M - R

X	DMC	¼X	B'ST
	blanc		
	300		
	304		
	315		
	316		
	321		
	340		
	341		
	347		*
	349		
	350		
	352		
	415		
	420		
	433		
	470		
	471		
	472		
	498		
	520		
	552		
	553		
	554		
	726		
	743		
	744		
	760		

X	DMC	¼X	B'ST
	761		†
	762		
	772		
	801		
	815		
	816		
	819		
	834		
	869		*
	898		*
	902		*
	918		
	920		
	921		
	934		
	935		
	937		
	938		
	963		
	3011		
	3012		
	3013		
	3045		
	3051		
	3051 &		
	3052		
	3052		

X	DMC	¼X	B'ST
	3053		
	3328		
	3345		
	3346		
	3347		
	3348		
	3350		
	3362		
	3363		
	3364		*
	3371		*
	3712		
	3716		
	3726		
	3727		*
	3746		

3371 French Knot

* For P, use 300. For N, use 347.
For R, use 902. For O, use 3350.
Use 3371 for all other.

† For R, use 938. Use 938 for all other.

* For P, use 935. For Q, use 937.
For R, use 934. Use 934 for all other.

▶ Use 1 strand of each floss color listed.

Projects shown on pages 44-47.
All project information on pages 90-91.

earth speaks in flowers

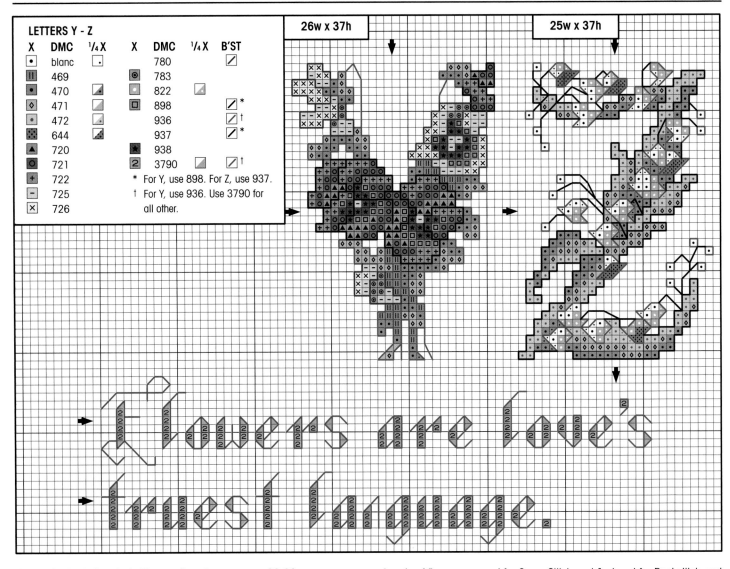

Charts for Earth Speaks in Flowers Sampler on pages 86-90.

Earth Speaks in Flowers Sampler in Frame (shown on page 45): The design was stitched over 2 fabric threads on a 17" x 26" piece of Cream Belfast Linen (32 ct). Two strands of floss were used for Cross Stitch and 1 strand for Backstitch and French Knots. Referring to photo for letter placement, align bottom edges of letters, leaving 4 squares between letters and 6 squares between lines; for verse placement, center verse horizontally 6 squares below alphabet, leaving 4 squares between words. It was custom framed.

Floral Monogram Porcelain Jar (shown on page 44): The letter "A" was stitched over 2 fabric threads on a 7" square of Cream Irish Linen (28 ct). Three strands of floss were used for Cross Stitch and 1 strand for Backstitch. It was inserted in the lid of a round porcelain jar (3½" dia. opening).

Floral Monogram Sweater (shown on page 46): The letter "H" was stitched over a 4" x 6" piece of 10 mesh waste canvas on a purchased sweater with top of design 2" below bottom of neckband. Four strands of floss were used for Cross Stitch, 2 strands for Backstitch, and 3 strands for French Knots. The letters "S" and "W" were each stitched ½" from the letter "H" over a 4" x 6" piece of 13 mesh waste canvas. Three strands of floss were used for Cross Stitch and 1 strand for Backstitch. See Working on Waste Canvas, page 56.

"LOVE" Pillow (shown on page 46): The word "LOVE" was stitched over 2 fabric threads on a 15" x 10" piece of Cream Belfast Linen (32 ct). Two

strands of floss were used for Cross Stitch and 1 strand for Backstitch and French Knots. Referring to photo for letter placement, align bottom edges of letters, leaving 4 squares between letters.

For pillow, you will need an 11" x 6" piece of fabric for backing, 5" x 62" fabric strip for ruffle (pieced as necessary), 34" length of ¼" dia. purchased cording with attached seam allowance, 62" length of 2"w lace, and polyester fiberfill.

Centering design, trim stitched piece to measure 11" x 6".

If needed, trim seam allowance of cording to ½"; pin cording to right side of stitched piece, making a ³⁄₈" clip in seam allowance of cording at corners. Ends of cording should overlap approximately 4". Turn overlapped ends of cording toward outside edge of stitched piece; baste cording to stitched piece.

For fabric and lace ruffle, press short edges of fabric strip ½" to wrong side. Press short edges of lace ½" to wrong side. Matching raw edges of fabric strip and straight edge of lace, machine baste layers together ½" from raw edges; gather to fit stitched piece. Matching raw edges, pin ruffle to right side of stitched piece, overlapping short edges ¼". Use a ½" seam allowance to sew ruffle to stitched piece.

Matching right sides and leaving an opening for turning, use a ½" seam allowance to sew stitched piece and backing fabric together. Trim seam allowances diagonally at corners; turn pillow right side out, carefully pushing corners outward. Stuff pillow with polyester fiberfill and blind stitch opening closed.

Floral Monogram Sachet Bag (shown on page 47): The letter "F" was stitched over 2 fabric threads on a 10" x 12" piece of Cream Cashel Linen® (28 ct). Three strands of floss were used for Cross Stitch and 1 strand for Backstitch and French Knots.

For sachet bag, you will need a 4½" x 7½" piece of Cashel Linen® for backing, 8" length of 1"w flat lace, 22" length of ¼"w ribbon, polyester fiberfill, and scented oil.

Trim stitched piece to measure 4½" x 7½", allowing 1¼" margins at sides and bottom of design and a 4" margin at top of design.

Matching right sides and leaving top edge open, use a ½" seam allowance to sew stitched piece and backing fabric together; trim seam allowances diagonally at corners. Turn top edge of bag ¼" to wrong side and press; turn ¼" to wrong side again and hem. Press short edges of lace ½" to wrong side. Blind stitch straight edge of lace to wrong side of top edge of bag; turn bag right side out and stuff with polyester fiberfill. Place a few drops of scented oil on a small amount of fiberfill and insert in bag. Tie ribbon in a bow around bag; trim ends as desired.

Floral Monogram Box (shown on page 47): The letter "B" was stitched over 2 fabric threads on an 8" square of Cream Cashel Linen® (28 ct). Three strands of floss were used for Cross Stitch and 1 strand for Backstitch. It was inserted in the lid of a 4½" square wooden box (3½" square opening).

Floral Alphabet Dresser Scarf (shown on page 47): The letters "J", "D", and "C" were stitched over 2 fabric threads across each short end of a 16" x 40" piece of Cream Cashel Linen® (28 ct). Three strands of floss were used for Cross Stitch and 1 strand for Backstitch. Referring to photo for letter placement, align bottom edges of letters, leaving 4 squares between each letter.

For dresser scarf, you will need two 16" lengths of 1"w flat lace.

On cross-stitched ends, match straight edge of lace to raw edge of fabric and use a ¼" seam allowance to sew lace to right side of fabric. Using a zigzag stitch to prevent fraying, sew close to seam; trim close to zigzag stitch. Press seam allowance to wrong side of dresser scarf. For remaining raw edges, turn fabric ¼" to wrong side and press; turn ¼" to wrong side again and hem.

Floral Monogram Album (shown on page 47): The letter "P" was stitched over 2 fabric threads on an 8" square of Cream Cashel Linen® (28 ct). Three strands of floss were used for Cross Stitch and 1 strand for Backstitch.

For photo album, you will need a 6¼" x 6½" photo album with a 2" spine, ½ yard of 44"w fabric, 15" x 6½" piece of batting for album, 4" x 5" piece of batting for stitched piece, two 5¾" x 6" pieces of poster board, 4" x 5" piece of adhesive mounting board, 12" length of 1"w

pre-gathered lace, tracing paper, pencil, and clear-drying craft glue.

Cut two 2" x 6½" strips of fabric. Glue one long edge of one strip ¼" under one long side of metal spine inside album; glue remaining edges of strip to album. Repeat with remaining strip and long side of metal spine; allow to dry.

Glue batting to outside of album. Cut a 17" x 8½" piece of fabric for outside of album. Center album, batting side down, on wrong side of fabric; fold fabric at corners to inside of album and glue in place. At center bottom of album, turn a 3" section of fabric ¼" to wrong side (**Fig. 1**); glue folded edge under spine of album. Repeat at center top of album. Fold remaining edges of fabric to inside of album and glue in place; allow to dry.

Fig. 1

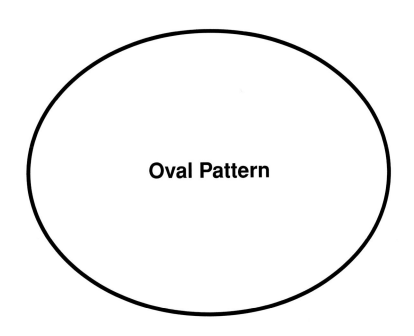

Cut two 6¾" x 7" pieces of fabric for inside covers. Center one piece of poster board on wrong side of one piece of fabric; fold edges of fabric to back of poster board and glue in place. Glue wrong side of covered poster board to inside of front cover of album approximately ¼" from top, bottom, and outside edges of album. Repeat with remaining piece of fabric and poster board for inside back cover.

For stitched piece, trace oval pattern onto tracing paper; cut out pattern. Draw around pattern once on mounting board and once on batting; cut out. Remove paper from mounting board and press batting piece onto mounting board.

Referring to photo, position pattern on wrong side of stitched piece; pin pattern in place. Cut stitched piece **1" larger** than pattern on all sides. Clip ½" into edge of stitched piece at ½" intervals. Center wrong side of stitched piece over batting on mounting board piece; fold edges of stitched piece to back of mounting board and glue in place.

Press short edges of lace ½" to wrong side. Beginning and ending at bottom center of stitched piece, glue straight edge of lace to wrong side of mounted stitched piece, overlapping ends of lace. Center and glue wrong side of mounted stitched piece to front of cover.

Oval Pattern

GARDEN OF INNOCENCE

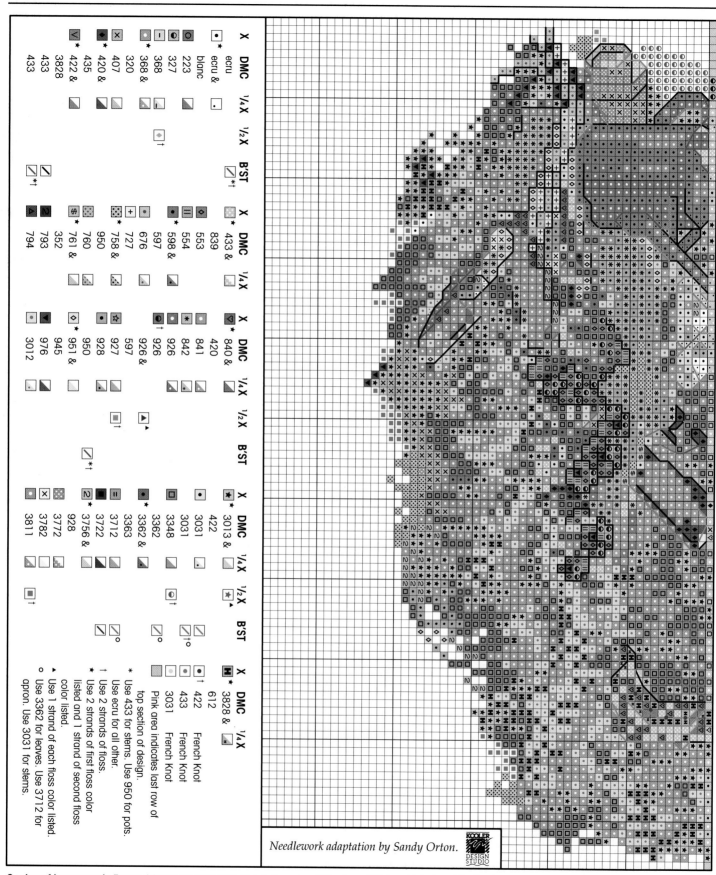

Needlework adaptation by Sandy Orton.

KOOLER DESIGN STUDIO

Garden of Innocence in Frame (shown on page 31): The design was stitched over 2 fabric threads on a 16" x 17" piece of Cream Cashel Linen® (28 ct). Three strands of floss were used for Cross Stitch, 2 strands for Half Cross Stitch, and 1 strand for Backstitch and French Knots, unless otherwise noted in the color key. It was custom framed.

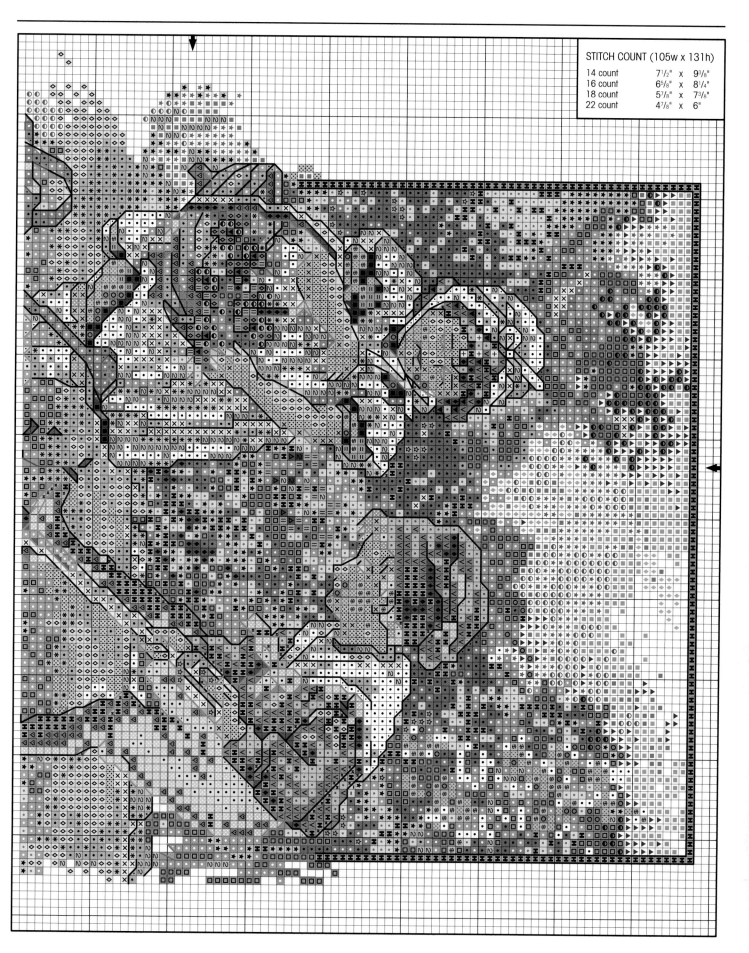

STITCH COUNT (105w x 131h)

14 count	7¹/₂"	x	9³/₈"
16 count	6⁵/₈"	x	8¹/₄"
18 count	5⁷/₈"	x	7³/₈"
22 count	4⁷/₈"	x	6"

GARDEN OF INNOCENCE

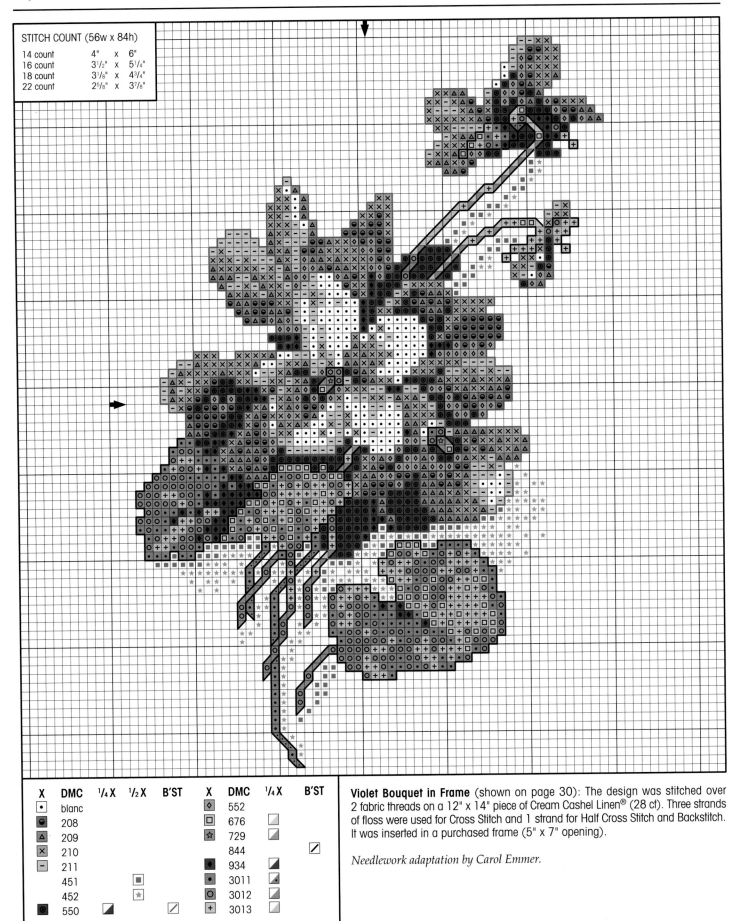

STITCH COUNT (56w x 84h)

14 count	4"	x	6"
16 count	3½"	x	5¼"
18 count	3⅛"	x	4¾"
22 count	2⅝"	x	3⅞"

X	DMC	¼ X	½ X	B'ST	X	DMC	¼ X	B'ST
•	blanc				◇	552		
◐	208				□	676	◰	
▲	209				☆	729	◲	
✕	210					844		◿
−	211				◆	934	◢	
	451		▣		•	3011	◢	
	452		★		◑	3012	◲	
◉	550	◿		◿	+	3013	◳	

Violet Bouquet in Frame (shown on page 30): The design was stitched over 2 fabric threads on a 12" x 14" piece of Cream Cashel Linen® (28 ct). Three strands of floss were used for Cross Stitch and 1 strand for Half Cross Stitch and Backstitch. It was inserted in a purchased frame (5" x 7" opening).

Needlework adaptation by Carol Emmer.

PICTURESQUE PANSIES

FINISHING INSTRUCTIONS

All of the following projects were stitched using individual pansies from the Wreath of Pansies Afghan design (chart on page 63).

Yellow Pansy Porcelain Jar (shown on page 16): A portion of the design (refer to photo) was stitched over 2 fabric threads on a 6" square of Cream Belfast Linen (32 ct). Two strands of floss were used for Cross Stitch and 1 strand for Backstitch. It was inserted in the lid of a round porcelain jar (2⁵/₈" dia. opening).

Tender Blooms Porcelain Jar (shown on page 12): A portion of the design (refer to photo) was stitched over 2 fabric threads on a 7" square of Antique White Cashel Linen® (28 ct). Three strands of floss were used for Cross Stitch and 1 strand for Backstitch. It was inserted in the lid of a round porcelain jar (3¹/₂" dia. opening).

Pansy Sachet Pillow (shown on page 16): A portion of the design (refer to photo) was stitched over 2 fabric threads on an 8" square of Cream Belfast Linen (32 ct). Two strands of floss were used for Cross Stitch and 1 strand for Backstitch.

For pillow, you will need a 4" x 4¹/₄" piece of Belfast Linen for backing, 34" length of 1"w flat lace, polyester fiberfill, and scented oil.

Centering design, trim stitched piece to measure 4" x 4¹/₄".

Press short edges of lace ¹/₂" to wrong side. Machine baste lace ¹/₄" from straight edge; gather lace to fit stitched piece. Matching gathered edge of lace with raw edge of fabric, baste lace to right side of stitched piece.

Matching right sides and leaving an opening for turning, use a ¹/₄" seam allowance to sew stitched piece and backing fabric together. Trim seam allowances diagonally at corners; turn sachet right side out, carefully pushing corners outward. Stuff sachet with polyester fiberfill; place a few drops of scented oil on a small amount of polyester fiberfill and insert in sachet. Blind stitch opening closed.

Picturesque Pansies Towel (shown on page 16): A portion of the design (refer to photo) was stitched over 2 fabric threads across one short end of a 13" x 20" piece of Cream Belfast Linen (32 ct). Center design horizontally with bottom of design 2" from short edge. Two strands of floss were used for Cross Stitch and 1 strand for Backstitch.

For towel, you will need a 26" length of 1"w flat lace.

Machine baste ¹/₄" from straight edge of lace; gather lace to fit short edge of fabric. On cross-stitched end, match gathered edge of lace to raw edge of fabric and use a ¹/₄" seam allowance to sew lace to right side of fabric. Using a zigzag stitch to prevent fraying, sew close to seam; trim close to zigzag stitch. Press seam allowance to wrong side of towel. For remaining raw edges, turn fabric ¹/₄" to wrong side and press; turn ¹/₄" to wrong side again and hem.

Pansies Basket Cloth (shown on page 16): A portion of the design (refer to photo) was stitched over 2 fabric threads in one corner of a 20" square of Cream Belfast Linen (32 ct) with design 1¹/₂" from raw edges of fabric. Two strands of floss were used for Cross Stitch and 1 strand for Backstitch.

For basket cloth, you will need 4¹/₂ yards of 1"w flat lace.

Press short edges of lace ¹/₂" to wrong side. Machine baste lace ¹/₄" from straight edge; gather lace to fit stitched piece. Match gathered edge of lace to raw edge of fabric and use a ¹/₄" seam allowance to sew lace to right side of fabric. Using a zigzag stitch to prevent fraying, sew close to seam; trim close to zigzag stitch. Press seam allowance to wrong side of basket cloth and topstitch close to edge.

GOLDEN SUMMER DAYS

FINISHING INSTRUCTIONS

Golden Sunflowers Pillow (shown on page 33, chart on page 78): For pillow, you will need a 7" x 18¹/₂" piece of lightweight fabric for lining, two 20" lengths of ¹/₂" dia. purchased cording with attached seam allowance, two 18" x 11" pieces of fabric for pillow front and back, and polyester fiberfill.

Centering design, trim stitched piece to measure 7" x 18¹/₂".

Note: Use a ¹/₂" seam allowance for all seams.

For band, matching right sides and short edges, fold stitched piece in half and sew short edges together. Press seam open and turn band right side out. Repeat for band lining.

If needed, trim seam allowance of cording to ¹/₂". Matching raw edges and beginning at seam, pin one length of cording to right side of one edge of band. Ends of cording should overlap approximately 1¹/₂". Turn overlapped ends of cording toward outside edge of band; baste cording to band. Repeat for remaining length of cording and edge of band. Matching right sides and seam, and leaving an opening for turning, sew band and lining together. Turn band right side out and blind stitch opening closed.

For pillow, match right sides and raw edges of pillow front and back. Leaving an opening for turning, sew fabric pieces together; trim seam allowances diagonally at corners. Turn pillow right side out, carefully pushing corners outward; stuff pillow lightly with polyester fiberfill and blind stitch opening closed.

Referring to photo, place band around pillow.

GENERAL INSTRUCTIONS

WORKING WITH CHARTS

How to Read Charts: Each of the designs is shown in chart form. Each colored square on the chart represents one Cross Stitch or one Half Cross Stitch. Each colored triangle on the chart represents one One-Quarter Stitch or one Three-Quarter Stitch. In some charts, reduced symbols are used to indicate One-Quarter Stitches (**Fig. 1**). **Fig. 2** and **Fig. 3** indicate Cross Stitch under Backstitch.

Fig. 1   **Fig. 2** 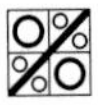   **Fig. 3**

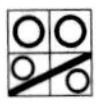

Black or colored dots on the chart represent Cross Stitch or French Knots. The black or colored straight lines on the chart indicate Backstitch. The symbol is omitted or reduced when a French Knot or Backstitch covers a square.

Each chart is accompanied by a color key. This key indicates the color of floss to use for each stitch on the chart. The headings on the color key are for Cross Stitch (**X**), DMC color number (**DMC**), One-Quarter Stitch (**¼X**), Three-Quarter Stitch (**¾X**), Half Cross Stitch (**½X**), and Backstitch (**B'ST**). Color key columns should be read vertically and horizontally to determine type of stitch and floss color. Some designs may include stitches worked with metallic thread, such as braid. The metallic thread may be blended with floss or used alone. If any metallic thread is used in a design, the color key will contain the necessary information.

STITCHING TIP

Working over Two Fabric Threads: Use the sewing method instead of the stab method when working over two fabric threads. To use the sewing method, keep your stitching hand on the right side of the fabric (instead of stabbing the fabric with the needle and taking your stitching hand to the back of the fabric to pick up the needle). With the sewing method, you take the needle down and up with one stroke instead of two. To add support to stitches, it is important that the first Cross Stitch be placed on the fabric with stitch 1-2 beginning and ending where a vertical fabric thread crosses over a horizontal fabric thread (**Fig. 4**). When the first stitch is in the correct position, the entire design will be placed properly, with vertical fabric threads supporting each stitch.

Fig. 4

STITCH DIAGRAMS

Note: Bring threaded needle up at 1 and all odd numbers and down at 2 and all even numbers.

Counted Cross Stitch (X): Work one Cross Stitch to correspond to each colored square on the chart. For horizontal rows, work stitches in two journeys (**Fig. 5**). For vertical rows, complete each stitch as shown (**Fig. 6**). When working over two fabric threads, work Cross Stitch as shown in **Fig. 7**. When the chart shows a Backstitch crossing a colored square (**Fig. 8**), a Cross Stitch should be worked first; then the Backstitch (**Fig. 13** or **14**) should be worked on top of the Cross Stitch.

Fig. 5   **Fig. 6**

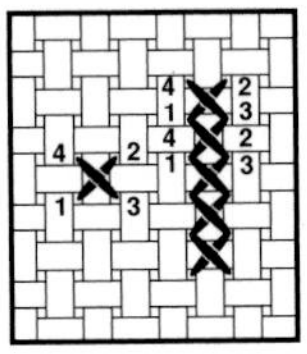

Fig. 7    **Fig. 8**

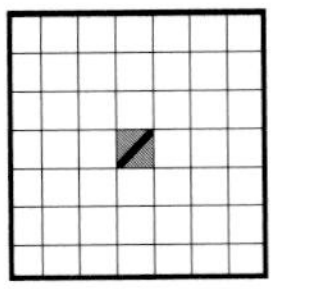

Quarter Stitch (¼X and ¾X): Quarter Stitches are denoted by triangular shapes of color on the chart and on the color key. For a One-Quarter Stitch, come up at 1 (**Fig. 9**), then split fabric thread to go down at 2. When stitches 1-4 are worked in the same color, the resulting stitch is called a Three-Quarter Stitch (**¾X**). **Fig. 10** shows the technique for Quarter Stitches when working over two fabric threads.

Fig. 9   **Fig. 10**

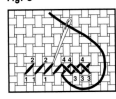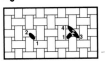

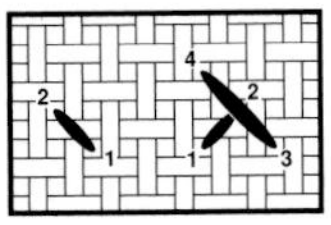

Half Cross Stitch (½X): This stitch is one journey of the Cross Stitch and is worked from lower left to upper right as shown in **Fig. 11**. When working over two fabric threads, work Half Cross Stitch as shown in **Fig. 12**.

Fig. 11   **Fig. 12**

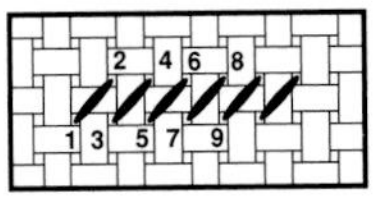

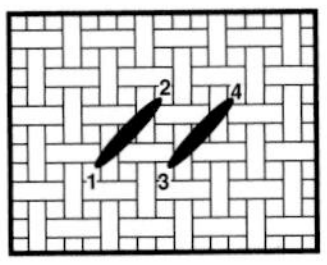

Backstitch (B'ST): For outline detail, Backstitch (shown on chart and on color key by black or colored straight lines) should be worked after the design has been completed (**Fig. 13**). When working over two fabric threads, work Backstitch as shown in **Fig. 14**.

Fig. 13   **Fig. 14**

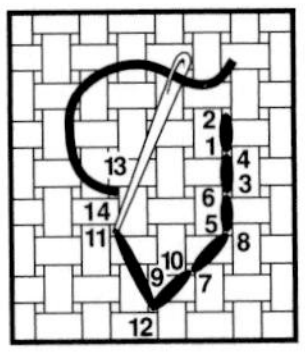

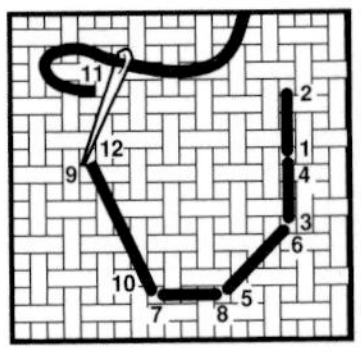

French Knot: Bring needle up at 1. Wrap floss once around needle and insert needle at 2, holding end of floss with non-stitching fingers (**Fig. 15**). Tighten knot, then pull needle through fabric, holding floss until it must be released. For larger knot, use more strands of floss; wrap only once.

Fig. 15

Couching: This stitch is composed of one long stitch held in place by short tie-down stitches (**Fig. 16**). Use two strands for long stitch and one strand same color floss for tie-down stitch.

Fig. 16

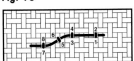

Instructions tested and photo items made by Arlene Allen, Lois Allen, Kandi Ashford, Vicky Bishop, Muriel Hicks, Pat Johnson, Arthur Jungnickel, Phyllis Lundy, Kelly Magoulick, Patricia O'Neil, Dave Ann Pennington, Angie Perryman, Stephanie Gail Sharp, Anne Simpson, Carolyn Smith, Trish Vines, Andrea Westbrook, and Sharon Woods.